Being Daoist

Being Daoist

順水之道

The Way of Drifting With the Current

Stuart Alve Olson

Valley Spirit Arts
Phoenix, Arizona

Copyright © 2014 by Stuart Alve Olson.

All rights reserved. No part of this publication may be reproduced or used in any form or by any means, electronic or mechanical, including photocopying, recording, or by any information storage and retrieval system, without the express written permission of the publisher except for the use of brief quotations in a book review.

Library of Congress Control Number: 2013949310

ISBN-13: 978-1-889633-14-5
ISBN-10: 1-889633-14-3

Valley Spirit Arts, LLC
www.valleyspiritarts.com

In loving memory of Master T.T. Liang
梁東材師
(1900 to 2002)

Photograph taken by Richard Peterson in Portland, Oregon, 1996.

This book is dedicated to Master T.T. Liang, my primary teacher and good friend. He showed me countless ways how to apply practical Daoism in my daily life, sometimes with humor and other times with great seriousness. This book is in so many ways a reflection and interpretation of my many years under his tutelage. It is my reverent hope this work does some justice to all he gave me.

Master Liang was one of the first teachers in the 1960s who brought taijiquan to America. His book *T'ai Chi Ch'uan for Health and Self-Defense* influenced thousands of Westerners to practice taijiquan. To learn more about him and his teachings, please see my book *Steal My Art: The Life and Times of Tai Chi Master T.T. Liang*.

A deified image of Lao Zi (老子).

Lao Zi is the attributed author of *The Scripture on Dao and Virtue* (道德經, *Dao De Jing*), the central foundational work of Daoism. Living in the sixth century BCE, his honorific and deified name is Tai Shang Lao Jun (太上老君, The Exalted One, Venerable Sovereign). Many Daoist texts credit him as the author under this name. The influence of Lao Zi's naturalist philosophy is a cornerstone of Chinese culture—socially, politically, and spiritually.

Acknowledgements

Many thanks to the following people who were so instrumental in helping make this book possible.

To my wife, Lily, who worked so extensively on my wording and meaning. I am so grateful for all her tireless efforts. She has given this book so much clarity and flow. Several times during the process of writing this book, I erroneously thought it done. But through her unrelenting persistence, motivated by a real hunger for clarity, this work underwent many revisions until reaching this version.

Many thanks to Patrick Gross, my longtime editor, friend, and student for enduring all the processes of change this book underwent, and for the seeming endless reformatting of the text.

Much appreciation must be given to Shi Jing and Shi Dao of the British Daoist Association. Their friendship and inspiration on being true Daoists has been very influential in my writing of this book.

To Professor Dave Capco, whose suggestions on the original draft brought about some wonderful and needed changes.

Many thanks must be given to Vern Peterson, my longtime friend who introduced me to Master Liang in 1981 and has always been a great advocate of my work. To John Orlando whose encouragement of what I teach and for the Sanctuary of Dao has been a true blessing. Likewise, much appreciation to Javier Grande who has been a constant pillar of support and benefactor for the Sanctuary of Dao. To Walter Melton, whose great friendship and interest in helping the Sanctuary of Dao grow has been truly remarkable.

Many thanks as well to Twila Gates, Ying Ying, Scott Reiland, Ken Johnson, Sherri Chastain, Bryant Seals, Laurie Battle, Denis Gendron, Bruce Goff, Jeff Upton, Dan Tilghman, Marguerite Mullins, Adam Sanders, and Sofi Shank.

To all my students who have so patiently sat through my ramblings on Daoist thought over the years, without them this book would never have been written.

Lastly, and most importantly, to my teacher Master T.T. Liang, without whom I would never have even thought to be on this journey of Dao.

To everyone I bow in deep gratitude.

Ancient Daoist Ode on Nourishing-Life Arts

Hearing the sound of flowing water nourishes the ears.

Seeing the green of trees and plants nourishes the eyes.

Studying books that explain principles nourishes the mind.

Playing the lute and practicing writing nourishes the fingers.

Wandering about on foot with a staff nourishes the feet.

Tranquility of mind and sitting in meditation nourishes your nature.

Harmonizing the qi nourishes the muscles and tendons.

Contents

Introduction 1
   Daoist Clergy and Priesthood Tradition 7
   Daoist Teacher and Disciple Tradition 11
   Daoist Scholars and Writers 18

Understanding the Way 27
   Personal Dao 31
   Virtue 37
   The Way 40
   The Naturally-Just-So 44

The Way of the Immortals 47
   Physical Immortality 49
   Longevity Immortal 54
   Spirit Immortality 55

The Way of Renewing Life 59
   Appreciation of Life 60
   Simplification of Life 66
   Transformation of Life 71

The Way of Wei Wu Wei	75
1) Active Non-Contention	79
2) Active Non-Interference	83
3) Active Non-Conformity	87
The Way of Sincerity, Silence, and Gentleness	91
Afterword	95
About the Author	97
About the Publisher	102
About the Sanctuary of Dao	103

Introduction

Nearly 2,500 years ago in a remote northwest corner of China, a man, departing from the ills and chaos of society, wrote a short book called the *Dao De Jing*. Advising people on how to live in harmony with nature and others, Lao Zi's words have silently spread throughout the world, like mist descending a mountain to fill the valley below. Though as apparent as mist, these simple words have proven just as difficult to grasp. Having become the basis of a religion, influencing great artists and poets, and generating thousands of other writings from learned people attempting to explain his seemingly simple words, the teachings of the *Dao De Jing* have culminated into what is now known as the philosophical and religious tradition of Daoism.

Many Westerners have been introduced to Daoism by reading one of the many translations of Lao Zi's *Scripture on Dao and Virtue* (道德經, *Dao De Jing*), or they have been exposed to it through the various Daoist arts that have filtered into our culture, such as feng shui, taijiquan, acupuncture, astrology, calligraphy, and so on. Because of Daoism's vast array of philosophical, spiritual, and health-related texts, no single work can serve as a definitive guide for Daoism. This is even more true given Daoism's long history and many branches of expression. So rather than trying to condense the whole of Daoism into one book, which would be impossible, the purpose of *Being Daoist* is to provide a practical interpretation on the basic philosophical ideals of living and thinking as a Daoist.

Learning to adapt Lao Zi's Three Treasures of kindness, frugality, and humility; through gaining knowledge of the terms Personal Dao, Virtue, The Way, and the Naturally-Just-So; learning to simplify, appreciate, and transform our life; gaining a clearer understanding of the term for immortality; in applying the principles of wei wu wei; and integrating the mindful actions of sincerity, silence, and gentleness—*Being Daoist* charts a clear path for seekers of the Dao to understand and find their Personal Dao, and for putting Daoist philosophy into action within our daily life. Daoism is a very dynamic philosophical teaching, it requires active participation within the processes of non-action. Meaning, a Daoist actively seeks to be as non-active as nature itself, doing without the strive of doing, wherein everything is then done naturally. The path for "being" Daoist is then the actions of blending in harmoniously with the world, imitating the doings of nature, and embracing the spirit within ourselves as true being.

In reading this work it should be understood that *Drifting With the Current* is not an expression about just letting go of all concerns or haplessly moving away from the world or yourself, it is a positive expression about drifting in a current of nonresistance back to our Original Spirit. The full statement of this in Chinese is *Push the Boat and Drift With the Current*. Pushing the boat is action, drifting is non-action. So in the context of being a Daoist, our practices and studies of Daosim are like pushing the boat into the current that will naturally and with great ease carry us back to our Original Spirit.

道

Before moving to the subject of actually "being" Daoist, it's helpful to have a perspective on how Daoism entered Western culture and some of the traditions it brought with it. Countless books on Daoist history explain its development in China, yet speak little about its introduction and assimilation into Western culture. I believe Western seekers of the Dao should have at least a sense of how Daoism has developed in the West and to pay homage to those who helped in the transition of Daoism to our culture.. When we read about the history of Daoism, it can seem so remote, like a figment or shadow, and so think it's not applicable to our current society and culture, that we cannot access the teachings and philosophy of it—which is simply not true. Daoism is growing in the West, and its history the United States, as well as in other countries, should not be passed over. So, examining how Daoism took root in the West is important for those of us attempting to nourish it and cultivate what will become known as Western Daoism.

The history of Daoism in the United States began in the mid-1800s with the Chinese who immigrated to California. Many of the Daoist temples they built are still standing today. Northern Creek Temple (北溪廟, Bei Xi Miao) in Marysville, for example, was built in 1854. Weaverville's Temple of the Forest Beneath the Clouds (雲林下廟, Yun Lin Xia Miao) was rebuilt in 1874 and is now part of California State Parks. In San Francisco's Chinatown, Heavenly Empress Temple (天后廟, Tian Hou Miao) and Dragon Palace (龍宮, Long Gong) were built in the mid-1800s. Terrace of Contemplation Temple (觀臺廟, Guan Tai Miao) in Mendocino is considered the oldest temple in rural California (built in 1854), and the Taoist Temple (道人廟, Dao Ren Miao) in Hanford was built in

1893. Hanford once had a population of Chinese greater than San Francisco.

Also during the mid-1800s, sinologists and Christian missionary scholars such as Frederic Henry Balfour and James Legge began translating Daoist texts into English. Other European sinologists such as Stanislas Julien, Herbert Giles, Lionel Giles, Richard Wilhelm, and Max Muller were translating Daoist texts into their respective languages as well.

Fast forward to the 1960s and people like Allan Watts and Gia-Fu Feng were writing about and teaching Daoism to the beat and hippy generation. During that period, Peter Goullart published his vivid account on Daoist life that he had experienced over thirty years of living in China.

Then in the early 1970s, John Blofeld started writing about his firsthand experiences of Daoist masters, teachings, and temples during his travels in the 1930s through late 1940s. His books brought Daoism to life in the West and inspired so many of us to become Daoists.

In 1974, photographer Hedda Morrison released a collection of her photos taken in the 1940s of Hua Shan and of the monks living there. These photos captivated and inspired many Daoist seekers in the West.

Once China opened up in the mid-1980s, many Westerners began traveling there to visit Daoist temples and seek out teachers. During this time various scholars and writers began presenting new Daoist works and the West started taking on a more serious approach to Daoism.

Additionally, Daoist ideals and thoughts have had enormous influences on some of the West's most accomplished writers and artists. Frank Lloyd Wright (1867–1959), one of the world's most notable architects, appears to have been greatly influenced by Daoist thought and art. What he called "Organic Architecture," a harmonious design approach for integrating buildings, furnishings, and surroundings with the natural world, mirrors the very basis of Daoist architecture. Within his architecture school, Taliesen West, you can see many Chinese works of art, as well as a quotes from the *Dao De Jing* painted on the wall.

Another famous figure in Western culture who helped in the propagation of Daoist thought was Carl Jung (1875–1961). As a psychiatrist and psychotherapist he found great influence in Daoist philosophy, even writing a foreword to Richard Willhelm's translation of the *Secret of the Golden Flower,* a work on Daoist alchemy and meditation. Many of the ideas he introduced into psychology were inspired by his studies of Daoist thought. On the nightstand next to his deathbed was a copy of *Chinese Meditations* by Lu Kuan Yu. Considering Jung's studies of Daoism and his tremendous influence on the field of psychology, his works introduced, sometimes indirectly, Daoist ideas and perspectives into Western society in a way that has had ripple effects throughout our culture.

Curiously enough one of the most influential sources of Daoist philosophy in Western culture was the television series *Kung Fu* starring David Carradine. The show, running from 1972 to 1975, introduced Daoist philosophy, both in word and action, to millions of Westerners. Even though the show was premised on a Buddhist Shaolin tradition, the main character, Kwai Chang Caine, was portrayed as, and exemplified, a wandering Daoist. The show relied on the Daoist philosophy of Lao Zi and Zhuang Zi to guide Caine's actions and thoughts. The *Kung Fu* series was the first actual depiction of a Chinese martial artist, yet showed little fighting. Caine is more often shown using Daoist philosophy to curtail and solve the problems he encounters rather than his martial skills. As the blind Master Po related to Caine once in the show, "Even a beautiful rose has thorns, but does not seek to use them."

Another major influence on Daoist thought in the West was Benjamin Hoff's *The Tao of Pooh* (Penguin Books, 1983), which remained on the *New York Times* Best Seller list for forty-nine weeks. Using the character of Winnie the Pooh as a Daoist master, Hoff presented many Daoist perspectives on living, which furthered a greater interest in Daoism, and, like *Kung Fu*, introduced Daoist teachings to people who weren't necessarily seeking to learn about Daoism.

In general, three main groups have been responsible for influencing and propagating Daoist teachings in the West, and they all approach the subject in numerous and varied ways.

The first group is the clergy, the ordained community of Daoists who engage in a rigorous training of disciplines determined by the particular sect to which they adhere. Ordained Daoists may or may not live in a monastery or temple, and they may or may not be celibate, as each sect of Daoism has its own requirements on these matters.

The second type of Daoist belongs to the teacher-disciple tradition and lineages, which in most cases are not of the clergy. This is truly the original way Daoism was taught and practiced by the majority of early Daoist cultivators.

The third group comprises the scholars and writers of Daoism. Whether these scholars and writers are or were

"Daoists" is irrelevant to the tremendous role they have played in strengthening and furthering the spread of Daoism around the world.

Daoist Clergy and Priesthood Tradition
The Chinese Taoist Association, founded in April 1957, is the one governing body for all Daoist sects. The association consists of two main branches: Zheng Yi (正一, The Correct One) and Quan Zhen (全真, Perfect Realization). All ordained Daoists are governed by one of these two sects, even if they belong to one or another of the twenty-eight subsects or chapters operating in China today. The Zheng Yi sect is headquartered at Dragon-Tiger Mountain (龍虎山, Long Hu Shan) in Jiangxi province, and the Quan Zhen sect at White Cloud Monastery (白雲觀, Bai Yun Guan) in Beijing.

The institution of the Daoist clergy began in 142 CE under Zhang Daoling (張道陵), whose sect became known as the Celestial Masters (天師, Tian Shi), but during a reformation period in the Tang dynasty (618–907 CE) the name Celestial Masters was changed to Zheng Yi. The Zheng Yi sect, generally speaking, favors the ritual and spirit work of Daoism more than the naturalist philosophy and tranquil meditation work of other Daoist traditions.

The Quan Zhen Sect began in the twelfth century under Wang Zhongyang (王重陽, 1113–1170 CE). In 1159, he learned from (through dreams and visions) the Daoist immortals Zhongli Quan and Lu Dongbin, the two founding members of the Eight Immortals (八仙, Ba Xian). The Quan Zhen sect, for the most part, embraces the philosophical and internal alchemy traditions of Daoism.

The traditional process for becoming a Daoist priest required the novice to first spend three years living in a temple, and only after accomplishing this was the novice allowed to undergo a one hundred day ordination ceremony, referred to in Daoist texts as "one hundred days of spiritual work," which included long periods of meditation, fasting, and other tests. This period of the ordination process was extremely harsh and brutal, sometimes resulting in death. When completing the spiritual work, the novice would undergo exams on Daoist scriptures, precepts, poetry, and chants. Upon passing the exams, the novice would be ordained as a priest, and would then be honored with the title of master (道師, Dao Shi, Master of the Dao).

During the Qing dynasty (1644–1912 CE) about two hundred novices every four years would be ordained. All ordination ceremonies were stopped in 1927 due to the turmoil taking place in China, but were resumed in 1989. The one hundred days of spiritual work was changed to fifty-three days to be far less severe. Now, depending on whether a person joins the Zheng Yi or Quan Zhen, the ordination requirements will vary as each sect has different criteria and focus.

Another interesting tradition in Daoism is the manner in which members of the clergy, the disciples, receive their spiritual name, or, as it is called, Dao Name (道名, Dao Ming). Traditionally, a teacher, or head of the sect, would choose a Daoist spiritual text or poem for determining the names of disciples, which would also indicate the generation of disciples to which they belonged. Each new disciple would then be given, in chronological order, one of the characters in the text. For example, let's suppose a teacher decided to use chapter 7 of the *Dao De Jing* to name new novices, and also decided to use Lu (路) as the surname (the family name of the sect) of all his students.

Chapter 7 of the *Dao De Jing* begins with the wording "tian chang di jiu (天長地久)." From this the first new disciple would be given the name Lu *Tian* (the first character in the text, 天). The second disciple would then be Lu *Chang* (the second character, 長), the third Lu *Di* (地), and the fourth Lu *Jiu* (久), and so on until all the names in the text were used. Then a teacher would select another text for his second generation of disciples. So from this system, the sect (family) name of the disciple and the generation a disciple belonged to could all be easily determined and recorded for posterity. In the Heavenly Masters Sect, for example, the surname of Zhang (張) was used, deriving from the founder Zhang Daoling.

In some cases, a disciple would later choose their own spiritual name, such as with Zhang Sanfeng. Sanfeng (三豐) means "Three Peaks," which refers to the three peaks he saw while cultivating and so named himself after he attained immortality. Before giving himself this name, legend has it that he was called Xuan Hua (玄化, Mysterious Transformation).

Apart from spiritual names, other indicators signify to which sect a Daoist disciple or priest belongs. The manner in which hand gestures (引手, yin shou) are used for salutations, how prostrations (拜, bai) are performed, how incense is offered (進香, jin xiang), and the design of ceremonial robes (禮服, li fu) and caps (冠, guan) are worn will vary among sects. The only general indicator of all Daoists is the wearing of the hair in a topknot (髻, ji), symbolic of wearing a crown, and many sects would even have specific hairpins (簪, zan), usually made of jade, ivory, or peach wood, for securing the topknot.

Many Westerners have been ordained as Daoist priests and many are undergoing the ordination process today. These dedicated individuals are helping to preserve and propagate orthodox Daoism all over the world. Without their efforts and influence, Daoism in the West could easily become a philosophical hodgepodge of either extreme intellectualism or erroneous personal ideologies. The ordained are in many ways a balance and measure between the academic and teacher-disciple traditions. It is crucial that the tradition of the Daoist clergy be maintained and supported so the teachings can be preserved for the growth and propagation of orthodox Daoism.

Suggested Reading:
- *Daoism in China: An Introduction* by Wang Yi'e (Floating World Editions, Inc., 2006).
- *The Daoist Monastic Manual: A Translation of the Fengdao Kejie* by Livia Kohn (Oxford University Press, 2004).
- *The Daoist Tradition: An Introduction* by Louis Komjathy (Bloomsbury Publishing, 2013).
- *The Taoist Body* by Kristofer Schipper (University of California Press, 1982).
- *The Taoists of Peking, 1800–1949: A Social History of Urban Clerics (Harvard East Asian Monographs)* by Vincent Goossaert (Harvard University Asia Center, 2007).
- *The Teachings and Practices of the Early Quanzhen Taoist Masters* by Stephen Eskildsen (State University of New York Press, 2004).

Daoist Teacher and Disciple Tradition

Before the time of Zhang Daoling, Daoism was taught through the medium of teacher and student/disciple lineages. This tradition continues today. Some teachers in present times may also be ordained Daoist priests, and some student/disciples may also be ordained. A student may be referred to as a disciple, apprentice, protégé, or adopted son or daughter. Traditionally, this group was primarily secular and usually pertained to teachers transmitting methods of internal alchemy (內丹, nei dan) and the practices of nourishing-life arts (養生術, yang sheng shu).

This form of teaching goes back to the time when Lao Zi[1] was departing society and met Guan Yin Zi (關尹子) along the border of China at the Northwest Passage. Guan Yin Zi persuaded Lao Zi to stay for a while to teach him the Dao, which resulted in Lao Zi writing the *Dao De Jing*.

The three primary ancestors of Daoism, who were the authors of the three foundational works forming Daoist philosophy, actually started the teacher-disciple tradition, certainly not by any intent to attract disciples, but through the merit of their works, which attracted followers. Together with

---

1   Lao Zi, a contemporary of Confucius, is said to have lived sometime during the sixth century (BCE). *The Scripture on Dao and Virtue* (道德經, *Dao De Jing*) has been attributed to him, which is probably one of the most translated and printed books in history. The main focus of the work is based on teachings of naturalism and non-contention. The overall context of his writings speak of the "unproduced," that all things are born from emptiness. The book consists of only five thousand characters in eighty-one concise chapters.

Lao Zi, Lie Yukou[2] (列圄寇, author of the *Lie Zi* [列子], thought to have lived in the fifth century BCE), and Zhuang Zhou[3] (莊周, author of the *Zhuang Zi* [莊子], who lived during the fourth century BCE) were the very founders of philosophical Daoism.

These three founders of Daoism were not part of a Daoist clergy—as Daoism would not be organized into a priesthood for many centuries after they lived and taught—but before and after their times, the teacher-disciple tradition existed. Indeed, there would be no Daoism, past or present, without this tradition. It is because of this personal transmission of knowledge and wisdom from one mind to another that is the heart of Daoism's extended history.

---

2   Lie Yukou's *Lie Zi* addresses the more mystical thought of Daoism, and it reflects the *Zhuang Zi's* thinking and style of writing. With the inclusion of Yang Zhu's writings (chapter 7 of the *Lei Zi*), the ideals of non-pretense, noninterference, free thinking, and free living are promoted.

3   Zhuang Zhou, author of the *Zhuang Zi*, is certainly one of China's greatest and most celebrated writers. Zhuang's writings centered on living in spontaneity (the naturally-just-so). Through stories, he speaks of the "unconditioned," that all things are illusory, such as his famous tale of dreaming he was a butterfly who was dreaming he was Zhuang Zhou. The book of *Zhuang Zi* consists of thirty-three chapters, but it is the first seven chapters, called the "Inner Chapters," that are considered the actual work of Zhuang Zhou. The remaining chapters are said to have been composed by his disciples and other writers.

INTRODUCTION

In Daoism this is called a "Mind" or "Heart Seal" (心引, Xin Yin). It is called a "seal" because the teacher affirms the student's realization of the true reality of the "oneness of being and non-being" through either word or action to seal it in the student's mind. In many ways this is a teacher melding his or her mind with the student's mind so the truth can be transmitted directly, with or without words. With this mind seal, the student is illuminated or awakened, and thus is able to attain and realize the Dao.

Ge Hong (葛洪, 283–343 CE), one of the most celebrated Daoist writers and internal alchemy cultivators, composed the *Master Who Embraces the Uncarved Wood* (抱朴子, *Bao Pu Zi*, Ge Hong's sobriquet), which is the first written record of a Daoist's personal search for immortality. Ge Hong was also not a member of the priesthood, rather he was part of the student/teacher tradition of Daoism. His great uncle Ge Xuan (葛玄), attributed author of the *The Exalted One's Clarity and Tranquility of the Constant Scripture* (太上清靜常經, *Tai Shang Qing Jing Chang Jing)*, played an important role in Ge Hong's interest in Daoism.

In more recent times, the famous 250-year-old man, Li Qingyun[4] (李青雲, reported to have been born in 1678 and died in 1933, with inquiries putting his age at 256), also received his teachings in the teacher-disciple tradition. Yet he

---

4 See *The Immortal: True Accounts of the 250-Year-Old Man, Li Qingyun* by Yang Sen, translated by Stuart Alve Olson (Valley Spirit Arts, 2014). A notice on Li Qingyun's death appeared in the *New York Times* on May 6, 1933, and in the *Time* magazine article "China: Tortoise-Pigeon-Dog," May 15, 1933.

chose not to give any information about his teacher, as some Daoists have done, other than saying he met his teacher in the Western Grotto Mountains in Gansu province.

The reason some Daoists do not offer personal details of their teachers is because they see no virtue in living off of a teacher's reputation and so seek to stand on their own worthiness and skills. This makes it difficult, however, to trace the lineages of many accomplished Daoist cultivators in the past.

Unlike the defined process for entering the priesthood, the teacher-disciple tradition can follow any number of paths. This is because the teachings imparted are purely up to the discretion of the teacher, and the teacher will teach a student according to the student's unique endowments.

In *The Classic on Transforming Barbarians* (化胡經, *Hua Hu Jing*), it states,

> A good teacher possesses the intuition to perceive a student's endowments and temperament, and so is able to determine whether a student should be taught the contemplative or sexual alchemy teachings.[5]

---

5   The *contemplative teachings* are broadly meant to include the philosophical, meditative, and nourishing-life practices of what is called "self-cultivation." The *sexual alchemy teachings,* on the other hand, refer to using sexual energy in practices of "dual cultivation." This term "dual cultivation," however, is applied differently within certain schools of Daoism as it can refer to a lone cultivator using sexual energy through self-stimulation along with internal alchemy, or to partner practices between males and females.

Introduction

The teacher-disciple tradition recognizes that not every student should be taught the same way, as people come into this world with different needs. As Master Liang said,

Some students who come to me can only learn the
health exercises, some only martial art, and a rare few
the way of becoming an immortal. So I must teach
each differently.

Not every student has the endowments or mental keenness to learn a teacher's entire art, yet all can benefit in one way or another. This way of teaching doesn't mean that a teacher's disciples acquired their learning any easier than a priest.

Many teachers required their students to endure long periods of sacrifice and training to earn their trust. In *The Yellow Emperor's Yin Convergence Scripture* (黃帝陰符經, *Huang Di Yin Fu Jing*), Chen Zhoutong (a disciple of Zhang Sanfeng in the Song dynasty) wrote this concluding remark to his commentary:

The Dao has been transmitted from sage to sage,
from ancestor to ancestor, and through this manner
the mental elucidation has been handed down. But,
presently, people erroneously think that uttering just
a few pleasant words of flattery to a teacher will get
them the transmission of Yin Convergence [immortality]
skills and consciousness.

These words by Chen Zhoutong have held true for teachers, past and present. Teachers in the past wanted to see sincerity, diligence, and respect in a potential student. Disciples who placed their teacher first, family second, and everyone else third understood that it was the teacher who enabled them to become immortal. And in becoming immortal, their family (ancestors and future descendants) would all benefit from the merit of their accomplishment. Parents, siblings, friends, or any other people in their life could not instruct them on the way of becoming an immortal. Therefore, the teacher played the most important role in a student's life. Teachers, be they spiritual or educational, were always held in high esteem in Chinese culture. This is not to say filial piety was not held in high regard as well. The basic thought is that parents nourish and give us life, and teachers give us wisdom and knowledge to understand life.

Regarding teachers in the West, however, a misnomer is often taking place, more specifically about those teachers who call themselves "master." In traditional Daoism, no teacher would ever have considered giving him or herself the title of master. It was up to the teacher's students to honor their teacher with this title because they felt it was deserved. An honorable and skilled teacher would never allow the title to be used unless granted by the students.

In the West, you'll find many self-appointed masters, which appears to be more a matter of self-aggrandizing and marketing than that of actual accomplishment. It would be wise for students interested in the teacher-disciple tradition to look carefully into whether the teacher or school of interest adheres to the traditional manners of giving and receiving the title of "master."

The teacher-disciple tradition, for the most part, is based on a personal approach to learning Daoism, whereas the ordained tradition is more about an institutional approach.

This is not to say novices or priests in the ordained tradition don't have personal relationships with their teacher or teachers, but the focus is more about following an established and formal system of learning through which each student must progress. In the teacher-disciple tradition, however, the learning and training is based on the needs and endowments of the student, with the teachings rooted in the deep empirical experiences of a teacher. The ordained/clerical approach is founded on the collected knowledge acquired from various sects and clergy in Daoism's long history. In the end, both traditions are crucial to Daoism's survival in the West as each provide a profound perspective on Daoism.

Suggested Reading:
- *The Monastery of Jade Mountain* by Peter Goullart (Llanerch Publishers, 1961).
- *Taoism: The Road to Immortality* by John Blofeld (Shambhala, 1978).
- *Taoist Health Exercise Book* by Da Liu (Perigee Books, 1974).
- *The Immortal: True Accounts of the 250-Year-Old Man, Li Qingyun* by Yang Sen, translated by Stuart Alve Olson (Valley Spirit Arts, 2014).
- *The Secret and Sublime: Taoist Mysteries and Magic* by John Blofeld (George Allen & Unwin Ltd., 1973).
- *The Story of Han Xiangzi: The Alchemical Adventures of a Daoist Immortal* by Yang Erzeng, translated by Philip Clart (University of Washington Press, 2007).

Daoist Scholars and Writers

Throughout Daoism's long history in China, including in contemporary times, numerous scholars have worked to preserve the history of Daoism and explain much of the voluminous literature collected since antiquity. This body of literature, called the Daoist Canon (道藏, Dao Zang), first compiled in 400 CE, consists of some fourteen hundred–plus texts of Daoism, including scriptures, discourses, commentaries, and instructional works. The Daoist Canon contains the writings of many Daoist adepts who either composed a scripture or wrote discourses on one aspect of Daoism or another, or simply provided commentaries on a previous scripture or discourse. In all, the Daoist Canon is a collection of writings created by, what may be called, true Daoist cultivators and masters, and it is these writings that Chinese scholars have been pouring over for centuries.

These pursuits have been echoed in the West, with numerous scholars, translators, and writers helping to present much of the Daoist Canon to their respective audiences. Without question this has been a tremendously valuable service to non-Chinese speaking Daoists.

Since Daoism was developed within Chinese culture, the language used in Daoist literature becomes extremely important. Daoism, however, uses many specialized terms and cryptic language, so being fluent in Chinese doesn't guarantee understanding every Daoist work. Few Daoist texts are worded in straightforward or colloquial Chinese. Much of Daoist literature is also steeped in mystical thought, making it difficult for the common Chinese reader to understand. So the works of scholars and writers on Daoism provide useful insights and clarity into source materials that most Western Daoists would not be able to interpret. Many of these works would not even be known, or even heard of, in the West if it wasn't for the efforts of these scholars and writers.

Most of the scholars and writers mentioned in this section have not been Daoists in the traditional sense nor engaged in the cultivation practices of the Dao, yet they have been an integral part of spreading Daoist teachings. Their efforts have been as crucial to Daoism's propagation in the West as have the efforts of the Daoist clergy and the teacher-disciple traditions.

For those of us Western converts to Daoism, and for those now undertaking the study of Daoism, the following author/translators and their works are how many of us came to learn about Daoism in the West. They have established the English literary foundation for all past, present, and future seekers of the Dao. It would be remiss not to recognize the likes of Frederic Henry Balfour, James Legge, Herbert Allen Giles, Lionel Giles, Henri Maspero, Lin Yutang, Holmes Welch, A. C. Graham, Hedda Morrison and Wolfram Eberhard, Burton Watson, Fung Yu-lan, Chang Chung-yuan, James Ware, Joseph Needham, Max Kaltenmark, Lu K'uan Yu, Gia-Fu Feng, Ilza Veith, Allan Watts, Chungliang Al Huang, Da Liu, and John Blofeld.

In more recent times, Thomas Cleary, Kristofer Schipper, Livia Kohn, Stephen R. Bokenkamp, Daniel Reid, Eva Wong, Michael Saso, Fabrizo Pedagio, and Isabelle Robinet are carrying on the tradition of scholarship and translation work.

All these pioneers and many more, have provided a framework, so to speak, for Daoist philosophy and practice in the West. The following books and periodicals are among the most popular and influential works on Daoism presented in English:

- *Alchemy, Medicine and Religion in the China of A.D. 320: The Nei P'ien of Ko Hung (Pao-p'u Tzu)*, translated by James R. Ware (M.I.T. Press, 1966).
- *Chuang Tzu: A New Selected Translation with an Exposition of the Philosophy of Kuo Hsiang*, translated by Fung Yu-lan (Commercial Press, 1933).
- *Chuang-tzu: Mystic, Moralist, and Social Reformer*, translated by Herbert Allen Giles (Kelly & Walsh, 1926).
- *Chuang-tzu: The Seven Inner Chapters and Other Writings from the Book Chuang Tzu*, translated by A. C. Graham (George Allen & Unwin, 1981).
- *Creativity and Taoism: A Study of Chinese Philosophy, Art and Poetry by Chung-Yuan Chang* (Harper & Row, 1970).
- *Early Daoist Scriptures,* translated by Stephen R. Bokenkamp (University of California Press, 1997).
- *Embrace Tiger, Return to Mountain: The Essence of T'ai Chi* by Al Chung-liang Huang (Real People Press, 1973).
- *Foundations of Internal Alchemy: The Taoist Practice of Neidan* by Wang Mu, translated by Fabrizio Pregadio (Golden Elixir Press, 2011).
- *Guarding the Three Treasures: The Chinese Way of Health* by Daniel Reid (Simon & Schuster, 1993).
- *Hua Shan. The Sacred Mountain in West China: Its Scenery, Monasteries, and Monks* by Hedda Morrison and Wolfram Eberhard (Vetch and Lee, 1973).
- *Lao Tzu and Taoism* by Max Kaltenmark, translated by Roger Greaves (Stanford University Press, 1969).

- *Science and Civilisation in China* by Joseph Needham (Cambridge University Press, 1954).
- *Tao Magic: The Secret Language of Diagrams and Calligraphy* by Laszlo Legeza (Thames & Hudson, 1973).
- *Tao Te Ching,* translated by Gia-Fu Feng and Jane English (Vintage Books, 1972).
- *Tao: The Watercourse Way* by Allan Watts (Pantheon, 1975).
- *Taoism: The Parting of the Way* by Holmes Welch (Beacon Press, 1957).
- *Taoist Meditation: The Mao Shan Tradition of Great Purity* by Isabelle Robinet, translated by Julian F. Pas and Norman J. Girardot (State University of New York Press, 1993).
- *Taoist Ritual in Chinese Society and History* by John Lagerwey (Macmillan Publishing Company, 1987).
- *Taoist Yoga: Alchemy and Immortality* by Lu K'uan Yu (Rider & Co., 1970).
- *The Book of Chuang Tzu,* translated by Martin Palmer (Penguin Books, 1996).
- *The Book of Lieh Tzu,* translated by A. C. Graham (John Murray, 1960).
- *The Complete Works of Chuang Tzu,* translated by Burton Watson (Columbia University Press, 1968).
- *The Divine Classic of Nan-Hua: Being the Works of Chuang Tsze, Taoist Philosopher,* translated by Frederic Henry Balfour (Kelly & Walsh, 1881).
- *The Dragon's Mouth* magazine (British Taoist Association, began publishing in 1996).
- *The Empty Vessel: The Journal of Daoist Philosophy and Practice* (Abode of the Eternal Dao, published quarterly since 1993).

- *The Sacred Books of China. The Texts of Taoism,* two volumes, translated by James Legge (Oxford University Press, 1891).
- *The Shambhala Guide to Taoism* by Eva Wong (Shambhala, 1997).
- *The Taoist Classics. The Collected Translations of Thomas Cleary Four-Volume Set* (Shambhala, 2004).
- *The Taoist Experience: An Anthology* by Livia Kohn (State University of New York Press, 1993).
- *The Way and Its Power: A Study of the Tao Te Ching and Its Place in Chinese Thought,* translated by Arthur Waley (Grove Press, 1926).
- *The Wisdom of Laotse,* translated and edited by Lin Yutang (The Modern Library, 1948).
- *The Yellow Emperor's Classic of Internal Medicine,* translated by Ilza Veith (University of California Press, 1972).
- *Workbook for Spiritual Development of All People* by Hua-Ching Ni (Shrine of the Eternal Breath of Tao, 1984).

This is but a partial list of some of the valuable Daoist works available in English, and I apologize for any other great books and authors I failed to mention. My intent was not to present an exhaustive list on the subject, but to provide a sampling of the numerous works that have been important in the propagation of Daoist teachings in the West (see also the other *Suggested Reading* sections for additional texts). Also keep in mind that many of the authors listed here have multiple publications to their credit.

道

INTRODUCTION

This brief introduction has attempted to explain how Daoism has entered Western society, showing how young it is in the West and how it is still trying to find its place within Western society and in these modern times. If you were to gather up all the writings and history of Daoism's development in China, and then compare it to what has occurred in the West, it would be akin to comparing a one hundred thousand–page book with a three-page article. In China, Daoism has at least three thousand years of history, but it has existed in the West for just over one hundred years.

When transitioning an old system into a new environment, disagreements and growing pains are bound to occur. The transition of Daoism into the West still has a long way to go, and how it will affect and find root in Western culture is still uncertain. We must all be cautious, however, not to practice elitism and cause a division between Daoist adherents.

My hope is that everyone involved in Daoism's transition and development into Western culture will see the great need for extending deep respect and support to all those who, in whatever fashion, help plant the seeds of Daoism. Whether it's the clergy, teacher-student lineage, or scholarly academic (both Daoist and non-Daoist), we all need each other, and it must be understood that we all perceive and love Daoism in our own way. If we can respect and accept the approach of these different sectors, then Daoism will blossom and thrive on Western soil.

If we consider Lao Zi's words "Contemplate the person by the person," then we should not judge or dismiss people by their race, creed, or nationality (or, in this case, by what sector of Daoism they follow). By extension, when we judge or dismiss others, contention is created. Here another statement of Lao Zi applies, "Sages do not contend with others; the inferior person is quarrelsome." A wise person (sage) sees no need or use in contending or quarreling with others, as it is only the unwise, inferior person who regards contention and quarreling as useful. So no matter which way we relate to Daoism—whether as clergy, teacher-student, scholar/writer, or as a person studying and practicing Daoism on their own through books and teachers—we must all practice Lao Zi's ideal of non-contention, otherwise we are undermining one of the central tenets of Daoist philosophy.

Daoism has a great opportunity to institute itself in the West, but it has to, at least in part, be adapted to Western culture. Changes are necessary and inevitable if Daoism is to survive and thrive in the West. As Western Daoists, we must clearly understand that a culture cannot just be stolen through imitation; rather we must learn and borrow from the past with reverence, while adapting the teachings to our culture through our own authentic experiences. This approach will allow us to nourish and develop a wonderful tradition of Daoism in the West.

Other teachers and organizations may define "Being Daoist" in different ways, and I do not contend with those views, for there are many perceptions of what it means to be Daoist. I wrote this book to summarize what my teachers and my many years of practicing, studying, and translating Daoist works have taught me on how to be Daoist. I make no pretense of claiming I know exactly what a Daoist is, nor that I am in any way a model of

Daoism. I am but one person, among many others, looking at a beautiful piece of art, and sharing my perception and experience of it. So much of Daoism I could not, in any practical sense, incorporate here. I am not an academic, nor would I dare call myself a master of the Dao, as there is simply too much about Daoism I don't know or have yet to accomplish. This book, then, should be regarded as but one droplet of water. Yet, I hope this droplet of water brings nourishment to some part of Daoism's developing roots in the West.

—Stuart Alve Olson

Understanding the Way

Following the Way, being Daoist, is about changing the negative characteristics of a person's temperament into good characteristics. The Daoist practices and benefits of meditation, taijiquan, qigong, and so on are limited unless a person transforms his or her thinking and conduct—this is to say, transforming delusion into wisdom. Lao Zi addresses this transformation in chapter 67 of the *Dao De Jing* where he reveals three principles for people to follow:

I have Three Treasures to hold and keep.
The first is called kindness.
The second is called frugality.
The third is called not daring to be first in the world.

Every human being, at heart, is a Daoist because every one of us intrinsically wants to live in peace and contentment. Lao Zi's advice on cultivating the Three Treasures of being kind, frugal, and humble allows us to do this by living in harmony with ourselves and the world. Lao Zi states in the same chapter,

> Kindness enables a person to be courageous.
> Frugality enables a person to be expansive.
> Not daring to be first in the world enables a person to grow into a full vessel.

Being kind applies both to yourself and to others. Daoists do not seek to change the world through big, bold actions, rather by showing kindness to those with whom they come into contact, and this takes courage. Showing kindness to others changes the world. Like a small stone tossed into a still pond, the ripples project across the entire surface.

Being frugal does not mean to be cheap, hoard wealth, or pinch pennies. In Daoism it means to be frugal about excesses, whether with food, pleasures, housing, clothing, vanities, business, and so on. So being frugal allows us to be expanding because we have retained the resources for doing so. Again, as Lao Zi points out, those who exhibit their wealth and treasures only encourage others to steal it. As he said, "Filling the hall with gold and jade, it cannot be protected" *(Dao De Jing,* chapter 9).

Being humble (not putting yourself first) is in many ways the hallmark of being Daoist. It helps prevent the three destructive behaviors of envy, avarice, and hatred from entering into your daily affairs and personality, and this allows us to grow to realize our full potential. When you put yourself first and do not consider the effects of your actions on others, you create the conditions for activating these three destructive behaviors. As Lao Zi states in chapter 66 of the *Dao De Jing,*

The Sage, in seeking to stay in front of others, must put himself behind them. Thus, the Sage stays in front of them.

This verse could equally be translated as, "Those who put themselves first end up last, and those who put themselves last end up first." Arrogantly acting as if you are better than anyone else, for example, only plants the seed of your own destruction. This is simply a law of nature.

Lao Zi's Three Treasures of kindness, frugality and humility are defining characteristics of the sage. Throughout the *Dao De Jing*, Lao Zi refers to the model of the sage. In some Daoist works this ideal is referred to as a "true person" or "realized person" (眞人, zhen ren), "immortal" (仙, xian), or "sage" (聖, sheng). No matter the title, the question remains what a sage really is.

In his book *The Monastery of Jade Mountain*, Peter Goullart provides a wonderful description of the sage:

> The Sage, as conceived by Laotse, is not, as some people may think, a mild, self-effacing and ineffectual weakling. Quite the contrary, he is a spiritual giant, but so wise and polished that he goes about amongst people without overawing or irritating them by his importance. He is square but he does not cut others. He himself is straight but he does not stretch others. He is angled but does not chip others and, although he is bright, he does not dazzle others. He leads but remains behind and though he is above people (by his intellect and virtue), he stays below them. He never wrangles with anybody and, therefore, no one likes to

wrangle with him. He is a saint but does not let people have an inkling of it. "Sainthood" is easy to conceal in Taoism as it does not differentiate between "clean" and "unclean" food and, as a matter of fact, does not mix religion with stomach. There are no ceremonial ablutions, mortification of flesh, prayers, public fasts or any other structures. Thus, the Sage is a mysterious, profound person, loaded with immense spiritual power and authority, who does not show it or speak of it. He is gentle, sweet, understanding, diplomatic, and can be a congenial and a true friend. No wonder his hierarchy has survived thousands of years and is still with us—unmolested, unsuppressed, and indestructible.

Human beings become sages by following the models of Heaven and Earth, the Dao, and the Naturally-Just-So. Although chapter 25 of the *Dao De Jing* may seem to be making distinctions between these terms, to model oneself after the Earth, by extension, means you are modeling yourself after Heaven, the Dao, and the Naturally-Just-So, as they are all connected:

Humanity models itself after the Earth.
Earth models itself after Heaven.
Heaven models itself after the Dao.
The Dao models itself after the "naturally-just-so."

Humanity modeling itself after the Earth means that people should understand and utilize the gifts of nature. Daoism, from its origins, has been a philosophy about learning to live naturally. Myriad practices have been created to obtain this way of life, as well as for achieving optimum health, longevity, and immortality. Undertaking Daoist practices, as well as following Lao Zi's Three Treasures of being kind, frugal, and humble, leads to being in harmony with nature, and is the way of the sage.

The four models of humanity, Earth, Heaven, and the Dao mentioned in chapter 25 of the *Dao De Jing* will be correspondingly examined further in the following sections on "Personal Dao," "Virtue," "The Way," and "Naturally-Just-So."

Personal Dao (自道, Zi Dao)

This term "Personal Dao" means to live according to a person's destined path in life. We all come into this world with certain endowments and affinities. When we find, connect with, and live our life according to these endowments and affinities, life flows more freely. We also feel whole and live life with purpose.

The question for most people is "How do I find my Dao, my natural path in life?" Finding the answer for some people may prove difficult, but for others it's easy. When you know your own self, seeing the path is clear. When you are perplexed and confused about your life, it's difficult.

Some of us are simply drawn to our path. No matter what we do or decide to do, the path keeps nudging us back to it. This means our affinity with a certain way of life will keep attracting our attention. Others of us are caught in confusion, mostly because we are stuck by conforming to what our family and society value, living our life in a pretense that leaves us unfulfilled.

The negative influences of politics, religion, and making a livelihood keep us constantly involved with the dictates of others. Politics can breed anger in us, religion can cause us to feel guilt, and business can drive us to be greedy. In the end, we feel no contentment about our lives.

In Daoism, the way to find your Personal Dao comes from contemplating the origin of your true self. This is accomplished by meditating upon your center of being, the Elixir Field (丹田, Dan Tian) in your lower abdomen, the very place of inception of life. Go back to your source and empty your mind. Answers come to those who give the body and mind space to receive them. Thomas Edison, when posed with a problem he couldn't resolve intellectually, would simply lie down on his couch and take a nap. Upon waking he would more often than not have the solution. This was his way of bringing clarity to the mind.

Many years ago I was acquainted with a fellow meditator who desperately wanted to find his path in life. He felt his family, girlfriend, and other friends were not offering the advice he needed and only served to confuse him more. Being a photographer simply wasn't making him feel whole or content in his life. He had asked the meditation master what to do. He was told, to his surprise, to just forget about it and simply meditate each day, to empty himself of this dilemma. So, twice every day he sat and just paid attention to his breath.

About three months later he pulled me aside after a meditation session and happily reported that he had found it. "Found what?" I asked, having completely forgotten about his dilemma. "My path," he said. He told me that a few days earlier he had realized while sitting that he wanted to become a scientist, which had never occurred to him until then. He was greatly interested in science ever since he was a young boy, yet it had never dawned on him to pursue a career in science until after this period of just meditating regularly on his breath. He claimed that the idea rushed into his consciousness so clearly and strongly that it couldn't be ignored. Soon after, he enrolled in a university and eventually graduated with a degree in science. Years later I heard from him and could clearly hear in his voice the contentment he had found.

There is both an Earthly (mundane) and Heavenly (spiritual) meaning to the term Personal Dao. Earthly Personal Dao is about finding and living according to your natural endowments. The Heavenly Personal Dao is about finding and living according to your inner spiritual destiny. In the *Yellow Court Scripture* (黃庭經, *Huang Ting Jing)*, a verse reads, "When the child is born it joins with the Milky Way." This has two meanings. First, we are not simply born into a family, a town or a country, we are born into the entire universe. We are part of, and join with, the entire cosmos. Second, and this has to do with spiritual cultivation, when we contemplate our true inner self (the Original Spirit) in meditation and awaken our lower Elixir Field (sensing the spiritual child within), we are released from the small box in which we are normally confined and become wholly aware of being connected to, and a part of, the universe. No longer are we just a mortal being shackled by boundaries and limitations. We sense an inner spiritual being unhindered by mortal constraints, and are aware of our place in the universe and the Dao.

This awareness of being part of the universe is our higher self, as opposed to the lower self which is trapped in the small box. The higher self is called the Hun (魂) spirit and the lower self, the Po (魄) spirit. The Hun spirit is a term denoting a person's Heavenly spirit, as well as the Three Primordial energies/spirits (三元, San Yuan) of a human being—a person's innate energies of jing (精, essence/body), qi (氣, vitality/breath), and shen (神, spirit/mind). The Po spirit is a person's more Earthly consciousness, and is also referred to as either the Seven Earthly Spirits (七魄, Qi Po) or as the Seven Emotions (七情, Qi Qing)—our mundane impulses. Collectively, these spirits can be thought of as our higher and lower selves.

Another view of this subject comes from looking at the division of Hun and Po spirits before we are born. While in our mother's womb, we are functioning completely within our Hun spirits; meaning, all our primordial energies are intact (our spirit, vitality, and essence), and this is our Before Heaven (innate) condition. Once we leave our mother's womb and the umbilical cord is cut, however, the Po spirits begin to develop and we are now in the After Heaven (non-innate) condition, where we must draw upon our natural endowments and nourish our minds and bodies so we may live according to our Personal Dao. In Daoism, the whole process of spiritual cultivation is to cut through the illusions and debris of the lower self (the Po spirits) to recapture the reality and clarity of the higher self (the Hun spirits).

People should always seek to follow their higher self. In every situation in our life we always have the opportunity to make a choice, a choice of doing what is right and best for ourselves and for others spiritually. So in Daoist terms, seeking out your Personal Dao would be a matter of realizing your Three Primordial (or Hun) spirits, and regulating the Seven

Emotions (or Po spirits). In Western terms, this means finding our higher self and lessening the hold of our lower self.

More often, however, we default to the yearnings of the lower self, making choices to appease our more immediate and pressing base desires. For example, a person who is discontent or suffering might turn to alcohol, drugs, sex, love, television, video games, Internet surfing, shopping, work, food, dieting, fanaticism, or obsession to numb or to escape from uncomfortable feelings. Instead we should trust we can handle the difficult emotions and situations, because if we numb the pain, we also numb our intuition and ability to access the real source of the problem.

It's crucial to make the decision to trust our higher self to find a more intuitive and less harmful solution to these situations. In the *Yellow Court Scripture* it says, "Move beyond yourself, soar high, and enter the Heavenly Road." *Entering the Heavenly Road* is a metaphor for those determined enough to choose to walk along their Personal Way (Dao).

Each of us has a conception of what our higher self is, and each of us knows on some level when we are submitting to our lower self. We are all capable of rationalizing our actions and can be unaware of how we so easily bend to the whims of the lower self. Sometimes we only know after the fact when we're suffering the consequences, but with mindfulness we can become self-aware enough in the moment to avoid letting the lower self drive us on autopilot. Be assured, however, that your Personal Dao only resides in your higher self. Just put your attention in your lower abdomen and empty your mind. Your higher self, your Hun spirit is right there before you.

Nothing is fixed about finding one's Personal Dao because we all come into this world with different fates and endowments, and none of us could engage at once in all the various practices and studies of Daoism that can lead to finding our Personal Dao. An old analogy about those who attempt to take on everything at once states, "Don't give an ant a watermelon and expect it to eat it in one bite." Daoist practices and studies are so far ranging and varied it would be impossible to study and practice them all. Wisely, some people choose to focus on one subject or a few subjects at a time until feeling ready to move on to other areas, or if they wish, to just stay with one teaching and focus solely on it for their whole lives. All that really matters is to be patient, constant, and resolute in a practice. It's better to master one thing than to be a jack of all trades.

In the long run, it doesn't really matter which of the practices and studies you choose to engage in, as they all overlap. Daoist practices and studies are usually divided into three gateways, namely the *philosophical* teachings, *nourishing-life* teachings, and *harmonizing yin and yang* teachings.

The *philosophical* teachings includes a vast array of studies deriving from the literature contained in the Daoist Canon, extending into the *Book of Changes* (易經, *Yi Jing)*, the spirit/ritual and ceremonial practices, and teachings on magic and talismans. The philosophical teachings center on the works of Lao Zi, Zhuang Zi, and Lie Zi, and they are primarily about acquiring wisdom. In Daoist terms, the philosophical teachings are about finding your Personal Dao and learning the way of Returning to the Source (Dao).

The *nourishing-life* teachings are, for the most part, physical practices designed to develop, both externally and internally, the energies of essence (jing), vitality (qi), and spirit (shen). These practices range from meditation techniques, numerous qigong exercises, taijiquan, and some styles of kung fu. Through these teachings, the means for restoring and developing health, youthfulness, and longevity are established and then extended into the methods of internal alchemy, the immortality teachings.

The *harmonizing yin and yang* teachings are primarily focused on the sexual methods in combination with internal alchemy. These teachings are typically referred to as "dual cultivation," as the majority of practices require a partner. In some cases, the term *dual cultivation* can also apply to individual practitioners who purposely incorporate the stimulation of their own sexual energy to heighten their progress in internal alchemy. So it is called "dual" because it is making use of sexual energy and contemplative absorption simultaneously. Daoism views sexual energy as the most powerful of all human energies, which when regulated and cultivated can be very useful towards the goal of obtaining immortality.

No matter if a person engages in the practices and studies of one gateway or all three, the most important aspect is to be sincere in whatever avenue of Daoist practice or study one undertakes. Without sincerity, there can be no good end or successful outcome of any of the teachings we undertake to find our Personal Dao.

Virtue (德, De)

In Daoism, the term for *virtue* holds a different meaning than what is found in English, where it is defined strictly as moral excellence and upright behavior. This is not to say that Daoism is void of teachings on moral excellence and upright behavior, but Daoists also recognize that forcing such behavior can be obstructive to living naturally and to freeing one's spirit. Religious fervor can bring about a fanaticism about behavior and morality that is very destructive. Lao Zi states that those who express their opinions (or beliefs) too strongly will become exactly what they oppose. This notion is rooted in the concept of extreme yang changing to yin, and extreme yin changing to yang. Just as day changes to night, and night into day. Therefore, Daoism's view is to temper the desire to do good and act correctly with a sense of following your intuition and Personal Dao, so that nothing becomes extreme.

The Daoist definition of virtue goes beyond morality and behavior as it denotes a spiritual power, energy, and influence. In a Daoist context, when a person is said to have virtue, this means he or she has successfully cultivated and achieved a spiritual illumination or awakening, and so has attained wisdom and a spiritual power or penetration (a spiritual skill).

In chapter 42 of the *Dao De Jing,* Lao Zi says, "Virtue follows the Dao." This means that the person of virtue embodies and exemplifies the Dao, and by extension draws upon the power of the Dao. Chapter 38 says,

> Those of high virtue are not virtuous, therefore they have virtue. Those of low virtue do not lose virtue, therefore they have no virtue. Those of high virtue do not act, for they have no cause for action. Those of low virtue act, for they have cause for action.

Lao Zi is saying that people who attain true and high virtue do not know of their high virtue, and so they really have virtue. Those of inferior virtue have nothing to lose because they actually have no virtue. Those with true or superior virtue have no reason or cause to acknowledge it, whereas those of inferior virtue proclaim their pretense of virtue so that they can benefit or profit from it.

Because the Chinese term for virtue (德, de) can be translated as "high spiritual power and influence," chapter 38 could be saying,

Those of high spiritual powers are unattached to
their spiritual powers; therefore, they maintain their
spiritual powers. Those of inferior spiritual powers
lose them because they become attached to just
exhibiting spiritual powers. Therefore, they really
have no spiritual powers. Those of high spiritual
powers do not seek to show them, because they have
no cause for doing so. Those of inferior spiritual skills
seek the pretense of skills, for they are attached to the
pretense of having skills.

Lao Zi also wrote in chapter 54, "When cultivating your own self, your virtue will be true." To "cultivate" means many things, including simply "to improve yourself." In Daoism, *cultivating virtue* means to nurture and strengthen your spirit, strengthening it so it becomes real and functional. It is virtue that brings forth the realization and illumination of your spirit, so that even upon death, the spirit functions with clarity. Virtue then, in Daosim, is considered the very power and energy for becoming an immortal, experiencing enlightenment, awakening to the Dao, or whatever one wishes to term it. So when a Daoist text says to "attain and realize," this is referring to attaining superior virtue so one can enter the Dao.

The Way (道, Dao)

No one with any authority can say exactly what a Daoist, Dao, or Daoism is. Lao Zi himself wouldn't define the Dao. When he says in chapter 25 of the *Dao De Jing*, "If pressed to give it a name, I would call it Dao," he was only providing an expedient means of talking about this subjective, undefinable force of nature. Lao Zi never even claimed he was a Daoist, at least not in the sense of being someone who adhered to any type of organized system of learning, religion, or established sect. Rather, he was just a "person of the Way."

Since there is no definitive definition of Dao, there can, by extension, be no definitive type of Daoist or practice of Daoism. The Chinese ideogram for Dao (道) shows a person drifting with the current along a watercourse way, going with the flow or following the natural course of things. This ideogram of Dao is a verb, expressing activity. Even though Dao is frequently used as a noun, it is really not correct to do so. Lao Zi used the ideogram Dao purely as an expedient term, but its proper use is active.

Daoism is China's first indigenous philosophical system, but in very early Chinese culture the practices of the shamans (巫醫, wu yi) and the method masters (方師, fang shi), along with a deep folklore tradition (concerning medicine, agriculture, and the spirit world) existed long before Daoism was organized. The philosophical tradition of Daoism did not begin until after the time of Lao Zi. Note I do not say "religion," as Daoism and Chinese culture in their traditional sense had no concept of religion. The Chinese had no word for religion until the advent of foreign missionaries.

In Daoist texts, four specific terms for understanding Dao occur: the *Constant Dao* (常道, Chang Dao), the *Perfect Dao* (至道, Zhi Dao), the *True Dao* (真道, Zhen Dao), and the *Great Dao* (大道, Da Dao).

The Constant Dao is the eternal and infinite nature of the Dao. The Constant Dao is not subject to the illusions of time and space. It cannot be calculated in time, nor can it be measured in size.

In the first chapter of the *Dao De Jing*, Lao Zi says, "The Dao that can be Dao*'ed* is not the Constant Dao." One explanation of this verse is that even if a person feels he or she is following the Dao, this action of following (cultivation) is still subject to the illusions of time and space. We humans, because of our rational thinking minds, put almost every action we perform into the context of "I." This "I" relies on forming the concepts of a life (time) and existence (space). In our rationale, if there is no time and space, there can be no "I," and without "I" there can be no following of the Dao. But Lao Zi states this is "not the Constant Dao." To make this clearer, look at how birds behave. A bird is just a bird, unaware of actually being a bird. There is no "I" with the bird, it is just being a bird. The bird does not seek out a method for being a bird. So, you could say it is the "Constant Bird." When we humans seek a Way to follow the Dao, we get our "I" into it, and this is not the Constant Dao. Get rid of this illusion of "I" and then there is the Constant Dao.

The Perfect Dao is the spontaneous and natural function of Dao, also called the "naturally-just-so." As Lao Zi states, "the Dao models itself on the naturally-just-so." Within Heaven and Earth are both good and evil, fortune and misfortune, but it is not the case that the Perfect Dao brings these about. As the first verse of *The Exalted One's Actions and Retribution Treatise* (太上感應偏, *Tai Shang Gan Ying Pian*) states, "There are no special gates through which misfortunes and good fortunes enter. We alone invite them in."

The Perfect Dao is like the sun. The sun doesn't choose who or what gets more light or more warmth, it just produces the light and warmth and everything is affected by it to varying degrees. The function of the Perfect Dao has nothing to do with creating the good and not-good, fortunes or misfortunes, the spiritual or mundane, these are all issues originating in the intents and actions of humanity. The Perfect Dao is just the workings of the naturally-just-so and it is considered "Perfect" because it responds to all things perfectly and equally.

The True Dao is the absolute reality of Dao that is not subject to any influences of Heaven and Earth, and not divided by *being/existence* (有, you) and *non-being/non-existence* (無, wu). It is not the "two," but the "one" (Dao). If the Dao were influenced by the activities of Heaven and Earth, it could not be the True Dao because it would then be divided by impulses favoring either Heaven or Earth, yin or yang,[6] and the good or not good. The True Dao is beyond all these dualities. It cannot be described in words because it is the One. No opposing influence or aspect can be compared with it.

The Great Dao means there is nothing beyond it and nothing that surpasses it, yet everything returns to it, even Heaven and Earth. The opening verse of *The Exalted One's Clarity and Tranquility of the Constant Scripture* remarks,

> The Great Dao is formless, yet it gave birth to Heaven and Earth. The Great Dao is without impulse, yet it revolves and gives motion to the sun and moon. The Great Dao is nameless, yet it eternally nourishes the myriad things. I do not know its name, but if pressed to give it a name, I would call it Dao.

The Great Dao is without a shape or image, yet from this formlessness all form is born, or in other words from nothingness comes all something*ness*. The Great Dao has no intent, desire, or impulse to cause any function of Heaven and Earth, yet all things naturally just do so because of it. The Great Dao has no name or label by which it can be described or pointed to, yet it is what sustains everything within Heaven and Earth. Lao Zi concludes this verse by expediently calling it Dao, but this is just a name, not a reality.

---

[6] Yin originally comes from the meaning of the "north" or "dark side of a hill," and later in Chinese philosophy was associated with the "female," "Earth," "dark," and "coldness." Yang originally comes from the meaning of the "south" or "sunlit side of a hill," and so is associated with the "male," "Heaven," "light," and "heat."

The Naturally-Just-So (自然, Zi Ran)

Daoism is based upon a philosophy of naturalism. Nothing in its view is beyond the influences of Heaven and Earth, except the Dao itself. As Lao Zi said, "The Dao models itself on the naturally-just-so." The naturally-just-so is the very spontaneous workings of nature and all phenomena. Constellations move and the smallest springs of life come forth because of the Dao. Thus, Dao is an active, formless, spontaneous, and unnamable force that operates all of nature, or as Daoists say, "Heaven and Earth."

> Contemplate the Dao of Heaven [nature], imitate the workings of Heaven, and all will be complete.
>
> *The Yellow Emperor's Yin Convergence Scripture*

To a Daoist, nature contains the solution to everything. To paraphrase a quote by Saint Augustine, "There are no miracles, just unknown laws of nature." Daoism has been unlocking these unknown laws of nature throughout its long history, developing some of the most effective natural means for promoting health, longevity, wisdom, and immortality through teachings on meditation, qigong, acupuncture, herbal medicines, internal alchemy, philosophy, feng shui, astrology, and more.

The "naturally-just-so" then is a matter of following, adapting to, and accepting the flow and changes of life. The universe and our very life function on this naturally-just-so. When we resist it, our life fills with turbidities and perplexities. So when we follow nature, when we adapt to nature, and accept nature, life flows much easier and the changes in life we encounter will no longer perplex us. Too often we fight with life and with nature, forever seeking to change both to our liking, but this only results in encountering more strife and harm. Embracing life and nature with the naturally-just-so is the actualization of contentment.

The Way of the Immortals

Any discussion of Daoism, especially regarding speaking on cultivating the Way of "being" Daoist, will eventually lead to the subject of immortality. Daoism, at its core, is a belief system in the existence of immortals and that the actual attainment of immortality is a potential within any person if he or she sincerely cultivates the Dao. However, Daoism maintains three distinct views on what immortality is—physical immortality (eternal youth), long-life immortality (living beyond one hundred years of age in good health), and spirit immortality (the body dies but the spirit of the individual remains conscious after death and beyond).

The Chinese term for immortal is *xian* (仙), an ideogram showing a person within a mountain, expressing the idea of hermits who leave society and worldly concerns to live in nature and cultivate their spirit in solitude. Many people who have written about their encounters with individual Daoist hermits or groups of Daoist hermits have commented on their joyous hospitality and friendliness. They describe the Daoist hermits as never shunning people of different religious or political beliefs, and purely accepting them as they are.

Sam Walter Foss must have been a Daoist at heart when he wrote "The House by the Side of the Road" because this poem best describes the nature of a true Daoist hermit:

There are hermit souls that live withdrawn
In the place of their self-content;
There are souls like stars, that dwell apart,
In a fellowless firmament;
There are pioneer souls that blaze their paths
Where highways never ran—
But let me live by the side of the road
And be a friend to man.

The concept of immortality is certainly not exclusive to Daoism, as many cultures throughout history have firmly believed in immortals and immortality as well. Ancient peoples of India, Greece, Scotland, Spain, and Scandinavia, for example, all accepted the existence of immortals. Chinese Daoists have maintained this belief since ancient times.

Daoism has long accepted and believed the answer to achieving immortality could be found in four distinct manners: 1) ingestion of specific herbs and plants, 2) refining certain metals and minerals into a pill of immortality, 3) diligent efforts of meditative internal alchemy, and 4) visitations from immortals who confer immortality upon the worthy.

In chapter 7 of the *Dao De Jing*, Lao Zi says,

Heaven lasts, Earth endures. They last and endure because they do not live for self and so they are able to be immortal.

This statement is a reference to achieving immortality by imitating the workings of nature (Heaven and Earth). In Daoism, this imitation means to attain clarity and tranquility. Clarity is represented by Heaven, and tranquility by Earth. These two attainments bring about immortality. This idea can be seen in the symbolic correlation of Heaven with the top of the head and Earth with the lower abdomen. When the top of the head and lower abdomen unite, this is, on a human level, the harmonizing and imitating of Heaven and Earth (nature), and thus a person (immortal) can live as long as Heaven and Earth. The key to achieving this immortality is to become selfless, which is none other than the attainment of clarity and tranquility. As it is says in the *Yin Convergence Scripture*, "Without self, what then dies?"

Physical Immortality

The first view of immortality is based on the premise of physical immortality, living forever in a physical state of youthfulness. Physical immortality shouldn't be dismissed as impossible. A species of jellyfish, Turritopsis nutricula, has been proven to be biologically capable of immortality.[7] This jellyfish can revert to its earlier polyp stage, effectively restarting its lifecycle and reversing the aging process.

Theoretically, Turritopsis can repeat this process indefinitely. Interestingly, "The Sleeping Immortal" poem by Zhang Sanfeng (Song dynasty, 1200 CE) mentions a Jellyfish Method:

The Sleeping Dragon[8] once rose up and ascended into
Heaven. It was he who transmitted this Jellyfish
Method.

Calling this transmission the Jellyfish Method is fascinating because it not only shows that Daoists equated jellyfish with immortality centuries ago, but that they knew this long before modern scientists discovered the ability of the Turritopsis species.

There are also cases of people in present times who have a mysteriously delayed aging process. According to a 2011 story on ABC News,[9] a six-year-old girl in Billings, Montana, still had the body of an infant. There is also a twenty-nine-year-old Florida man who has the body of a ten-year-old boy, and a

---

7 Piraino, Stefano, et al. "Reversing the Life Cycle: Medusae Transforming into Polyps and Cell Transdifferentiation in Turritopsis nutricula (Cnidaria, Hydrozoa)," *The Biological Bulletin* 190 (June, 1996): 302–312.

8 *The Sleeping Dragon* is a moniker for Zhang Guolao (張果老), one of the Eight Immortals.

9 See "Benjamin Button Children Never Grow or Age" by Susan Donaldson James *(ABC News)*.

thirty-one-year-old Brazilian woman who has maintained the body of a two-year-old girl.

Although these cases are clearly not the immortality that Daoism professes, and are certainly not desirable states of being for these people or their families, these examples demonstrate that nature is not fixed when it comes to aging.

In chapter 2 of the *Master Who Embraces the Uncarved Wood*, Ge Hong expounds on the reasons for the belief and acceptance of immorality and immortals:

What we know [of immortals] could never equal the
bulk of what we don't know [of them]. What possibly
is there in creation of all myriad forms that does not
exist? Why then should immortals, whose histories fill
our books, somehow not exist? Why should there then
be no divine process that can guide us to attain
immortality?

In the same chapter, Ge Hong says, "Just because you do not see ghosts, spirits, and immortals, doesn't mean you can know with certainty they don't exist."

He presents a good argument here because many examples in history of beliefs that people couldn't prove later turned out to be true. In the fourteenth century, for example, the majority of people believed the world was flat. People also never thought it possible to communicate instantly with others, even if on the other side of the earth, but now it is commonplace. Going to the moon and beyond, discoveries of effective cures for various diseases and ailments, and even flying around the world in airplanes were all just considered fantasy and impossible a little over a hundred years ago.

We believe in many things we can't actually see, and accept those things purely on faith. We put forth faith on life itself, even though our future is nothing but hopeful imagination. We experience and feel emotions, but can't see them. People who say they don't believe in things they can't see and touch might first consider the function of their imagination, because everything in their life is a product of imagination. The car they drive, the house they live in, the job they hold, all were originally just a thought. Everything that now exists was at some point not real, not until the thought of it first occurred.

As the *Yin Convergence Scripture* states, "Everything is created and destroyed by mind." Thoughts themselves cannot be seen, heard, tasted, smelled, or touched, yet we accept that thoughts are real.

Many of our beliefs are confirmed in our minds by the Five Senses (sight, sound, taste, smell, and touch), yet everything we experience and sense through these Five Senses is nothing more than an illusory, mentally created perception, not a true reality of what is being sensed. For example, some object may be laying upon the ground. One person may see it as a stick, another person may observe it as a snake, another as a crack in the ground, another as a shadow, and another may not see anything at all. So how is it some people can make the claim, "I will only believe it if I can see it with my own two eyes?" They should equally claim this about their thoughts and their identity as these can't be seen with the eyes, so how could they possibly believe in them?

This is why the *Yin Convergence Scripture* also explains that these Five Senses are just Five Thieves—because they steal from us the clarity of true seeing, robbing us of the consciousnesses of the sense organs. Each sense organ has a physical organ (eyes, ears, tongue, nose, and skin), and each has a function (seeing, hearing, tasting, smelling, and touching). But these organs and functions each have a consciousness (a mental energy or intuition) as well. Again, the *Yin Convergence Scripture* states, "The deaf person can see well, and a blind person can hear well." This is because when a sense organ and its function are taken away, the consciousness of the organ and function remains intact and actually increases the energy and intuition of that sense. True seeing, true hearing, true tasting, true smelling, and true touching have nothing to do with either the physical organ or the function of it, as each function can only provide us with illusionary perceptions created purely from external stimuli, and so reality becomes a false perception of accepting what we can physically see, hear, taste, smell, or touch.

We accept as real what we can confirm through our senses. We believe in mortality because we have bodies that age and die. People do not believe in physical immortality because it can't be verified by the senses. Although we can imagine this state of being, proving that immortality exists lies beyond our sensory perception. This division between accepting the seen and rejecting the unseen is viewed by Daoists as shortsighted and reveals a mind affected by the Five Thieves. A true Daoist accepts the seen and unseen equally, and accepts mortality and immortality equally, as everything has its yin and yang nature.

Longevity Immortal

The second view of immortality in Daoism is actually about the attainment of longevity, to live life to the fullest potential, preserving youthfulness within old age, and living beyond one hundred years of age. But the attainment of longevity requires cultivation of one's internal energies as well as a conscious belief in the ability to extend the life span, because if it is not in the mind it cannot be realized in the body. In our youth we feel immortal, but we lose that sense because we come to fully accept aging and death, thus resigning ourselves to this inevitable conclusion of mortality. Most people pay no attention to the restoration of youthfulness throughout their lives. Long-term bad eating habits, excessive dissipation of physical and sexual energy, constant striving, anxiety concerning financial and survival issues, and unmindful expression of the Seven Emotions are all like a self-perpetuating wheel racing towards death. Few people know how to get off the wheel, even if we recognize we are on it. This is mostly because we have created a culture that profits from our conformity. We ignore the ideas of simplifying our life, and forego setting our own path because it's too hard to go against the norm on a day-to-day basis.

Most people are active and enthusiastic about life at an early age, but then accept and settle into a rote way of existence until their death. As Benjamin Franklin put it, "Most people die at age twenty-five, but aren't buried until they're seventy-five."

Daoism likewise addresses this problem with the idea that youthfulness can be maintained even into old age—professing that we need not assume old age equals having one foot in the grave. My teacher would humorously state, "Johnny Walker: the older the better."

Daoists don't consider old age as undesirable because they maintain their youthfulness as they age. Just thinking like a young person doesn't mean you will never die, but youthful thinking can change the quality of your life. Children laugh and smile many times each day; older people do so just a few times each day. Children seek to play, and adults seek to survive. Without laughter, smiles, and play we become old. Embracing a youthful attitude and outlook helps you become and stay youthful.

The Chinese have a greeting, "May you have youthfulness in old age." This is certainly a worthwhile goal for any person. To maintain good health, agility, sexual vitality, and a clear mind even into old age is then not old age at all. It is very much like being immortal, just as we felt in our adolescence.

Spirit Immortality

The third and most predominant view of immortality in Daoism is the immortalization of one's spirit—meaning, to live on in spirit form after physical death. Immortalizing the spirit is the goal of most practices of nourishing-life arts and internal alchemy methods. Most of the practices rely on the processes for accumulating and refining the energies of jing (essence/body), qi (vitality/breath), and shen (mind/spirit).

Immortalizing the spirit seems to be the goal of most Daoist teachings on self-cultivation. The process may be called "Illuminating the Spirit" (神明, Shen Ming), "Awakening the

True" (悟真, Wu Zhen), "Realizing the Original Spirit" (悟元神, Wu Yuan Shen), or "Returning to the Source" (還源, Huan Yuan), to name a few. No matter the terms used, and there are many, all these refer to cultivating various practices to strengthen the spirit enough so it is "realized" and can exist and function in ethereal form beyond death. In Daoism, the majority of venerated spiritual beings and immortals were once mortal. Each immortal had a mortal existence and through self-cultivation gained immortality and spiritual powers.

Apart from those who achieved immortality through self-cultivation, many tales in Daoist folklore are about various gods and goddesses in the Chinese pantheon who did not practice self-cultivation to achieve their immortality. These were people who were deemed worthy or had performed good deeds or made great sacrifices for humanity and were thus rewarded with immortality by an existing immortal or immortals.

Daoism classifies immortals into three ranks, or types. *The Immortals Classic* (仙經, *Xian Jing*) states, "The cultivators of the highest rank can raise their bodies into the Void and are called Heavenly immortals (天仙, Tian xian)." Usually these Heavenly immortals are described in Daoist tales as mounting a crane or dragon and ascending into the empyrean, maintaining the state of eternal youth. Heavenly immortals are usually deified at some point and may hold some official post in Heaven.

Those of the second type shed their bodies after death and are called "corpse-freed immortals" (尸解仙, shi jie xian). These types of immortals have no more use for living in a physical body and so they no longer seek to undergo being reborn into the world, preferring to ascend into an immortal paradise to live in spirit form. Corpse-freed immortals are usually equated with their mortal counterpart, cloud wanderers, as their actions simulate each other—with the cloud wanderer roaming high mountains and the corpse-freed immortal roaming immortal paradises.

Those of the third order retreat into a reputable high mountain and are called "Earthly immortals" (地仙, Di xian). Earthly immortals are thought to live one hundred years or more, and will choose their time of death, doing so peacefully. Not all Earthly immortals retreat to the mountains. Some choose to remain in society to maintain obligations or to teach. The Earthly immortal is usually viewed as a "longevity immortal," and will return to an Earthly existence to continue his or her cultivation of immortality.

To conclude this subject on Daoism and immortality, it's best to quote the eloquent words of John Blofeld from his book *Taoism: The Road to Immortality* (Shambhala, 1978). This quote perfectly captures the Daoist meaning and quest of an immortal:

> An immortal is one who, by employing to the full all his endowments of body and mind, by shedding passion and eradicating all but the simplest and most harmless desires, has attained to free, spontaneous existence—a being so nearly perfect that his body is but a husk or receptacle of pure spirit. He has undergone a spiritual rebirth, broken free from the shackles of illusionary selfhood and came face to face with his "true self," aware that it is not his personal possession, being no other than the sublime undifferentiated Tao! With the vanishing of his seeming ego, he sees himself no longer as an individual, but as the unchanging Tao embodied in

a transient cloud-like form. Death, when it comes, will be for him no more than the casting off of a worn robe. He has won to eternal life and is ready to plunge back into the limitless ocean of pure being!

Suggested Reading:

- *A Gallery of Chinese Immortals: Selected Biographies Translated from Chinese Sources,* edited by Lionel Giles (John Murray, 1948).

The Way of Renewing Life

The foundation of cultivating wisdom, longevity, and immortality relies on paying attention to the three renewing processes of appreciating, simplifying, and transforming one's life. Methods will be empty and limited unless we first put forth the effort to truly change certain aspects of our temperament and perceptions of life. Being a Daoist is about the acceptance of change and the determination for renewal. A famous bathtub dating from the Shang dynasty (1600–1046 BCE) had this inscription on its side, "Renew, renew, and renew again. Every day renew!" We must, as the bathtub proclaims, change and renew every day until we can transform and enter the Dao. *Change,* in the context of cultivating the Dao, means to accept and adapt to the fluctuations in your life, as certain changes can lead to transformation. *Renewal* means to adopt those changes that can bring transformation. In this way, a new fullness and appreciation of what life can be is realized. Acceptance and appreciation are like the two legs supporting your cultivation of immortality. All cultivators of the Dao should contemplate this question, "If I am not a realized immortal right at this moment, how then can I possibly not feel that cultivating change and renewal is necessary?"

When we don't appreciate our life, for example, we may feel perplexed, and when perplexed, our meditation skills will be unfocused. A life that's too complicated can create confusion, which hinders true insight (intuition and mindfulness). When we avoid seeking to transform our life, we are stuck in conformity and dullness. We then have no hope of changing mortality to immortality. So living life by these three renewals is invaluable for drawing out the spiritual power of virtue, culminating in attainment of the Dao.

Appreciation of Life

Too often we forget how incredible it is to be alive. We gasp and cling to our first breaths coming into this world, then we take it for granted for most of our life, and then gasp and cling to it again right before death. We more often than not take our life and breath for granted and only pay attention to them when they are threatened. Daoism teaches us to appreciate the life we have and each breath we take. Breathing is life, because without breath we have no qi,[10] and without qi we have no life.

---

10 Qi is defined as "breath," but is also "the energy that animates and preserves life." Therefore, the definition of qi covers a wide range of meanings, such as "vital-life energy," "internal heat" (the warmth of body is dependent on qi), "a steam-like vapor for mobilization of blood," "internal power," "an inherent oxygen in the blood," and "a potential externally expressed power."

To sit in meditation, focusing the breath in the lower abdomen, and bringing a fullness to the breath, is one of the highest acts of appreciating life we can perform. Taking our breath for granted is to take life for granted. An inhalation is no guarantee of an exhalation, a day is not a guarantee of a night, and life is no guarantee of truly living.

Daoists understand that the emotions of being happy or sad, experiencing love or hate, and the feelings associated with gain and loss are all a part of being mortal. To be mortal is to experience emotions. But Daoism also recognizes there is a difference between those emotions having control over you and you having control over your emotions. For example, we can experience the emotion of love, yet we also need to guard against the emotions of love developing into a negative experience, such as becoming addicted (or, in Daoist terms, attached) to the high of being in love and/or codependent on others. Love may then become a springboard for anger or an illusionary replacement for what we feel is missing in our life, as some people are more in love with the idea of being in love than really being in love.

Being in love, as wonderful as it is, can produce negative emotions when losing that love. When experiencing the loss of someone we love, for example, we naturally feel sorrow and grief, which are important emotions to feel within the healing process. Problems develop, however, when we cling to the sorrow or grief.

The *Zhuang Zi* tells a story about a student who goes to pay his respects to his teacher, Zhuang Zhou, whose wife had recently passed away. When the student enters the courtyard of his teacher's home, he finds his teacher beating on a drum, singing, and laughing. The student considers this inappropriate and questions him on his behavior.

Zhuang Zhou responded that at first he felt sorrow for the loss of his wife, but then soon realized that the sorrow was purely his emotion, a reaction to his loss. He further reflected that her birth and life were celebrated, so why not her death? Adding that she originally came from the Dao and was now just returning to it, so why should this not be an occasion for celebration? Zhuang Zhou found no wisdom in clinging to his sorrow; rather he found good reason to feel joy for his wife's return to the Dao.

This story illustrates how Zhuang Zhou used wisdom to be mindful of his emotions and thereby turned the conditions of sorrow over his wife's death into the condition of joy for his wife's return to the Dao. Zhuang Zhou saw his initial sorrow as exclusively his emotional reaction to his loss, and in the end expressed joy for her gain.

All feelings associated with the events in our lives should be experienced with some degree of equanimity because all will turn to their opposite in time. No one can be in a constant state of happiness, as one of the other emotions will eventually take over. There is nothing fixed about the Seven Emotions (happiness, anger, sorrow, fear, grief, anxiety, and love/lust) we experience. They are erratic and as subject to change as the wind. For example, we can laugh so hard we can cry at the same time. We can be so angry over not being loved that we simultaneously push love away. We can be so much in love that many more things about the object of that love can anger us.

Any of the Seven Emotions in the extreme will naturally transfer itself to yet another emotion. It is for this reason Daoism teaches us to be constantly mindful of our emotions because when any of them become extreme, they literally become the destroyers of our tranquility, clarity, contentment, and spiritual illumination. All emotions can be experienced in either a positive (yang) or negative (yin) condition, just as there is yin within the yang and yang within yin.

If we cannot see misfortune and good fortune as both producing and reflecting each other, and if we cannot see them as merely momentary experiences, then we cannot truly appreciate life because life is a fluctuation of opposites. Appreciating life does not mean only to favor the good fortune that comes into our life, but equally to accept and understand the misfortunes as well. Just as daytime and nighttime follow each other, we should appreciate the opposites of all things if we are to ever experience harmony, peace, and contentment in our life.

Again, as stated in *The Exalted One's Actions and Retribution Treatise*, "There are no special gates through which misfortunes and good fortunes enter. We alone invite them in." We should not blame others for our misfortunes, nor should we praise ourselves (by being arrogant or boastful) for our good fortunes. Both fortune and misfortune are a result of our past actions and thoughts. We identified with the result and, therefore, it came about. It is far too easy to lay our successes at our own feet, but lay our failures at the feet of others. This is not appreciating life, as we can only do so when we realize life is not about being praised or extending blame to others. It is far better to gratefully accept our good points and seek to correct our bad points.

None of this means we can't be proud of our successes or feel dismay over our failures. What it does mean is that we should not boast of our successes, as this will only cause others to feel incompetent and less fortunate, plus it sets up conditions for others to feel envious and resentful. So, boasting of good fortune and success will, in turn, create misfortune. Conversely, blaming others for our misfortunes or failures creates the conditions for others to become angry and seek revenge. It is best to quietly accept misfortune and failure with an attitude of rectifying the problem. Daoism teaches personal acceptance of both good fortune and misfortune equally because fortunes change, and we should understand that within good fortune there is misfortune, and within misfortune there is good fortune.

When you change your focus, explicitly bringing your focus on what you are grateful for, even if it seems like things are going poorly and you are in the midst of suffering and loss, you will find much to appreciate in your life. Sometimes we are so centered on what we don't have that we completely forget about what we do have. Just to be alive as a human being should be cause enough for great appreciation of life. Lao Zi wrote,

When following the Dao, you identify with the Dao.
When following virtue, you identify with virtue.
By identifying with the Dao, the Dao will gladly
accept you. By identifying with virtue, virtue gladly
accepts you. When you identify with loss, loss will
gladly accept you too. *(Dao De Jing,* chapter 23.)

When accepting and identifying with the Dao (both the universal and Personal Dao), the Dao will provide what you need to resolve your problems. This is not a process of asking the Dao for anything or to engage in wishful thinking, rather it's an acknowledgement of the root powers of the Dao. You are an integral part of the Dao, so everything you need is within you. You are Dao, and Dao is you. Look to your own virtue, your own inner power and influence to resolve the matter. Too often we forget that there is a power (which can be called a spirit) within each of us to manifest not only our destiny but also the solutions to troubles and problems. Keep in mind that reacting negatively is not necessary, as we are all capable of expanding our ability to act consciously when confronted with a problem. It just takes mindfulness and practice. We are capable of so much, but more often than not we backslide into melancholy, panic, and fear when faced with a trouble or problem.

An old Daoist adage states, "Heaven is gentle to those who follow their Dao." This could also be translated as, "Nature is kind to those who follow their Way." Those who follow their Personal Dao are doing what their intuition and higher selves know to be right, thus the Dao is with them. It is so simple, yet it protects itself from being discovered by those who do not seek their Dao.

Whenever students expressed a negative view about some situation in their life, Master Liang would always say, "Life is beautiful and you are wonderful." He understood that we all have a choice in any given situation or environment to either see the beauty or ugliness in it, and Daoists strive to appreciate whatever situation in which they find themselves—regardless of whether it provides fortune or misfortune. They can do this because they see that everything we encounter and experience is nothing more than a lesson or guide along our path, our destiny. We can either choose to let these encounters and experiences anger or depress us, or we can choose to learn from them and, thereby, feel appreciative and grateful for the lesson.

Simplification of Life

The Daoist idea of simplifying life is accomplished by seeking and attaining contentment, practicing nonconformity, and regulating the Seven Emotions of happiness, anger, sorrow, fear, grief, anxiety, and love/lust. Feeling discontented with our lives, being a conformist, and allowing our Seven Emotions to express themselves to the extreme are what make our lives so excessively complicated.

Simplifying Life by Seeking Contentment

It's easier to add to your life than to subtract and simplify, but making your life simpler is key to being content. Daoists do not look for happiness, as they consider happiness like catching a cold. Happiness is just an emotion, subject to change. Contentment, on the other hand, is a consistent state of being, a state of perception, and a conscious choice, like being in a state of gratitude. For the uncultivated person, contentment can easily be lost because of external factors, but for the cultivated person contentment comes from within and therefore is a constant.

Contentment means living in joyful gratitude. The joy comes from being unfettered by anxiety and striving, and the gratitude from living according to who and what we are. Happiness, being one of the Seven Emotions and subject to change, is something we have to guard against attaching to. By living in contentment, Daoists are able to tread the Seven Emotions without the extreme highs and lows. We may find contentment even in suffering, but no one can make a conscious choice to experience happiness whenever they wish. We can pretend to be happy, but that is not the true experience of happiness.

Daoists do not attach themselves to happiness because they know it cannot last. Happiness is like a wave that comes and goes. By not grasping onto it and being attached, Daoists are able to simply be grateful for the experience they had, whether, "good" or "bad." By not chasing highs and running away from lows, Daoists are able to experience contentment. This is what Zhuang Zi meant in his famous quote "Contentment is the absence of the striving for happiness."[11]

Simplifying Life Through Nonconformity
Daoists do not conform to the societal demands of excessive materialism or maintaining social reputations. Life is much more stressful and complicated when we want what everyone else has

---

11 Translating this quote as *"Happiness is the absence of the striving for happiness"* is incorrect from a Daoist standpoint because "happiness" is one of the Seven Emotions and, therefore, a Daoist would never strive for it. In this statement, Zhuang Zi uses the ideograms of *an le* (安樂) to mean "contentment" (literally "joyfully content") and *xi* (喜) for "happiness" (the same ideogram for happiness used in the listing of the Seven Emotions). So the mistranslation is understandable from a common point of view, but incorrect when considering the Daoist perspective and meaning.

and when we strive to appear normal, if not better, than everyone else. Nonconformity is an essential way to simplify one's life.

In present times we more often than not see celebrities, politicians, and people in the entertainment world acting with self-absorption, extravagance, and arrogance. They are simply conforming to what they think they need to do to get attention and to be relevant. But they are only a form of entertainment that thrives on drama. They are actually models of how to have a complicated life. We cannot simplify our lives by following such examples. Nonconformists think and act by their own intuition, not by how others tell them to act or think.

Many influences in our society make us feel like we must conform, especially pressures from those who want us to conform to justify their beliefs and life choices. Conforming then only leads to generating further conformity. True nonconformists, on the other hand, want others to experience the freedom to be themselves, so their words and actions only serve to help people to see their own mind and find their own way, nothing more. Great artists, for example, don't tell people how to interpret their work. They create from their own intuition and spirit and let people think of it what they will.

So to be a true nonconformist, you must learn to trust your own intuition and make use of your own endowments. Nonconformity is not about being a rebel or thinking that other people's beliefs are wrong. True nonconformity is purely about being true to yourself and allowing others to be who they are.

Simplifying Life by Regulating the Seven Emotions

The Seven Emotions can often be sources of overcomplicating our lives. Many times when our lives are chaotic on the outside it is because we have a chaotic emotional landscape on the inside. Our external worlds are very much a reflection of our internal states.

Most of the time, emotions are good for us. We need them for our interactions with other people. But when they become extreme, they will fuel negative mental states and behaviors. As mentioned, happiness can lead to sadness when the source of our happiness disappears. Justifiable anger can quickly escalate into rage, sorrow can lead to melancholy, fear can lead to madness, grief to depression, anxiety to psychosis, and lust/love can turn into addiction.

One of the most important aspects of regulating these Seven Emotions is to take responsibility for them. Taking responsibility for our emotions is the first step in learning how to regulate them and simplify our lives. It does very little good to blame others for your irritability, outbursts, or rage expressed at them. An old Chinese saying goes, "You can see the faults of others quite clearly, but cannot see the dirt on the back of your own neck."

It is so easy to direct our anger at others and not see our own role in the situation. This outward expression of anger is usually more about an anger we have toward ourselves. We just redirect the anger at others because we find it too difficult to look at the real source of the problem.

The solutions to these extreme experiences of the emotions are mindfulness and being kind to ourselves. Through a regular practice of mindfulness and self-reflection, eventually there develops a natural response of calmness and clarity within any situation. No one, according to Daoism, is doomed by these Seven Emotions. Keep in mind these are also called the Seven Qi because each emotion is an energy, so just as we can regulate our breath (qi), we can equally regulate our emotional responses to situations. First we must train ourselves to be aware of and observe our thoughts and emotions as they arise. By becoming aware of our emotions, noticing how they are affecting us and not judging them, as well as being kind to ourselves, we begin to create a space where they no longer define who we are in that moment. We can see that our thoughts are not facts and our emotions are not reality—they are simply our thoughts and emotions.

When we realize we can be in the moment, feel our emotions, and accept them into our lives with kindness and understanding, they lose their power over us. As Carl Jung said, "That which we resist, persists." So once we stop trying to fight and run away from our emotions, they are less overwhelming. From being aware and accepting of ourselves and our emotions, over time we become more able to make conscious choices and respond positively in a situation rather than react defensively.

Keep in mind, Daoism is not about eliminating the Seven Emotions, but about the calming of them so they don't interfere with the processes of attaining clarity, tranquility, and immortality. To be human is to have emotions, and Daoism only views them as problematic when they become extreme and lead us away from contentment and cultivation. Learning how to work through emotions in a healthy way is an important part of cultivation and an essential way to simplify your life. Imagine how content your life could be if you were not constantly undergoing the anxieties and perplexities created by the Seven Emotions. The gateway to this freedom is acceptance, mindfulness, and being kind to yourself, your emotions, others, the world, and life in general.

Transformation of Life

Transformation carries two meanings in Daoism: 1) To attain and realize the Dao. 2) To follow your Personal Dao. In the first meaning, transformation occurs from a sincere cultivation of longevity and immortality teachings. In the second sense, transformation occurs from a sincere determination to let your intuition guide you and not conform to the dictates of others and society. Ultimately, both ways of transformation are about changing from a mortal into an immortal.

Lao Zi discusses transformation in the *Clarity and Tranquility Scripture*:

> Even though it is called "Attaining the Dao," in truth there is nothing to attain. It is only because of the transformation of a person that it is called "Attaining the Dao."

Attaining this "transformation" is what Daoists seek. Leaving the world for the high secluded mountains is not a prerequisite for practicing or obtaining the Dao. The Dao can be obtained right where you are. Transformation can occur within lowly settings or magnificent ones. It is purely about changing the mind, and mind is the only place where the Dao can be obtained. In Daoism, transformation may be considered as the realization of your immortal self while also seeing the false trappings of the mortal self. Transformation means to become selfless, and being selfless is the gateway of becoming an immortal.

Countless stories in Daoism talk about people who left their worldly duties to follow the Dao (Lao Zi himself did) and live without all the stresses of common life. Some became "cloud wanderers" (雲旅, yun lu), simply wandering the mountains and living in nature. Some built or joined a hermitage or temple in which to live and cultivate, and some literally followed Lao Zi's advice in chapter 47 of the *Dao De Jing* and stayed at home to cultivate:

> Without going out your own door, one can know
> the whole world. Without looking out your window,
> one can see the Dao of Heaven. The farther one
> goes, the less one knows. Therefore, the Sage knows
> without going.

All Daoists, from past to present, seek to transform themselves, whether to enter into the Dao or find their Personal Dao. Sometimes, however, the way of going about this appears contradictory. Lao Zi, for example, left society, yet he implied that to find the Dao, you need not go out your own front door or look out your own window. Does this mean we need to isolate ourselves from society, or cultivate right where we are?

Lao Zi was not seeking transformation when he left for the Northwest Passage. He was already transformed. He, like so many other Daoist immortals, was simply seeking peace in which to cultivate further to Return to the Source (Dao). So leaving the world to enter the solitude of the mountains was really meant for those who have already *realized the Dao* and obtained a transformation. Not "going out your own door," then, is a statement for those who are cultivating to transform themselves and to follow their Personal Dao.

In Daoism, the process for transforming into an immortal involves the study and cultivation of what is called "internal alchemy" (內丹, nei dan). These immortality teachings are predicated almost entirely on a metaphorical perception; the perception of the creation of an internal spiritual (immortal) child—a means by which to experience transformation through one's Original Spirit (元神, Yuan Shen).

Internal alchemy has various methods of development and practice. The simplest way to explain it is by first stating that everyone comes into this world with the prenatal components of generative force (jing), vital energy (qi), and spirit energy (shen), collectively known as the Three Treasures.[12]

The combined strength of these three components is what fuels the process of transformation into an immortal. However, because they are the energies of our body, breath, and mind, we deplete and diminish our Three Treasures through our Seven Emotions and mortal desires. Daoists, then, practice internal alchemy to replenish their Three Treasures, thereby setting up the foundation to attain and realize their Original Spirit. In other words, awaken their immortal spirit.

Original Spirit is the very essence of our spirit. It is what we were even before we entered our mother's womb. This is

---

[12] The Three Treasures of jing, qi, and shen refer to the energies of body, breath, and mind. They are unrelated to Lao Zi's Three Treasures of kindness, frugality, and humility.

why it is said "there is nothing to obtain," because Original Spirit is something we already possess but haven't recognized yet, and transformation is the recognition of our Original Spirit. So it is not that the Dao is unobtainable, we just need to acquire deep clarity and tranquility to see it.

Internal alchemy is a way of acquiring this clarity and tranquility to undergo the transformation from mortality to immortality.

The Way of Wei Wu Wei

Whereas learning to appreciate, simplify, and transform your life is really a matter of personal learning and cultivation, this chapter on the Daoist principle of active non-action is primarily about interactions with others.

In my many years of teaching taijiquan, I frequently hear students say how relaxing it feels to perform the taijiquan solo form, but once they are introduced to the partner exercises, they immediately become resistant and tense. Living as a Daoist is similar, because being Daoist is not just a matter of interacting with yourself, but interacting with others as well. Being Daoist is the ability to respond and interact with the world through the Daoist ideal of *wei wu wei* (active non-action).

Lao Zi said, "Acting through non-action [wei wu wei], there is nothing left undone" *(Dao De Jing,* chapter 3). This active non-action, or "non-doing," is at the heart of all Daoist practices and philosophy, yet it is one of the most misunderstood principles of Lao Zi's teachings.

Lao Zi wasn't advising that people do nothing. Rather he was encouraging us to have a mindset of being active while not attaching ourselves to the actual doing of the task, not feeling the task is work or drudgery, or becoming stressed about the task and feeling disgruntled about it. What Lao Zi is implying is that we should approach all our actions with a mind of perfect freedom, no matter the task at hand. We do many active non-actions every day because they're things we love or enjoy, and so we have no thoughts of them being a task. However, when we have a task we judge to be a drudgery, such as mowing the lawn, we add layers of mental strife on top of the task instead of just being in the moment with it.

Simply said, wei wu wei is an act of mindfulness free of anxiety within any task. The Dao is in everything, even in things we don't like doing—so, seen in this light, everything we do is a means of cultivating the Dao. But the meaning of wei wu wei goes much further than this.

Lao Zi's concept of "active non-doing" includes three ideals of conduct for interacting with others and the world. They are a reference for those who seek to follow Lao Zi's philosophy of wei wu wei. However, these three ideals are difficult to maintain, as they are contrary to the responses we normally experience from the conditioning of the Three Poisons, Six Sense Desires, and Seven Emotions.[13]

The underlying theme of the *Dao De Jing*, for instance, focuses on the ideal of non-contention, while the *Zhuang Zi* and *Lie Zi* (especially the writings of Yang Zhu contained within it) emphasize noninterference and nonconformity. These three ideals of non-contention, noninterference, and nonconformity are the very expressions of wei wu wei for interacting with others.

Understanding how to apply these active non-actions is not a theoretical practice, as non-contention, noninterference, and nonconformity are important practices of mindfulness in our day-to-day conduct. Applying the ideals of wei-wu-wei entails both the active element of being mindful and the non-active

---

13 The *Three Poisons* (三毒, San Du) represent the three negative characteristics of greed, hatred, and delusion, which relate to the three Elixir Field (Dan Tian) areas of the body. Greed comes from the stomach (lower Elixir Field), hatred from the heart (middle Elixir Field), and delusion from the brain (upper Elixir Field). Greed creates gluttony and lust, hatred nourishes all the negative perceptions, and delusion produces dullness and confusion. The Daoist ideal is to turn these Three Poisons into the *Three Medicines;* meaning, turning greed into giving and charity, hatred into kindness and compassion, and delusion into wisdom and understanding. *Six Sense Desires* (六慾, Liu Yu) refer to the objects we desire and attach to from what we see, hear, smell, taste, touch, and think about. *Seven Emotions* (七情, Qi Qing) refer to the feelings of happiness, sorrow, anger, anxiety, fear, grief, and love/lust. Rather than being controlled by the Three Poisons, Six Sense Desires, and Seven Emotions (the normal condition for humanity), Daoists "turn the conditions" through active non-action (wei wu wei).

element of guarding against a negative response. Throughout the day issues may arise that create conditions for conflict. Active non-action does not mean doing nothing. It means actively guarding against expressing the negative responses of contention, interference, or conformity. By recognizing when potentially negative situations arise, we can consciously choose to react in a more positive way.

Lao Zi alludes to the difficulty (and the reality) of applying the ideals of wei wu wei in chapter 70 of the *Dao De Jing:*

> My words are very easy to understand, and very easy to put into practice. But the world does not understand them, nor put them into practice.

Most translations of this verse read, "But no one can understand them and no one can put them into practice," which is a rather defeatist perception of Daoism and misinterpretation of Lao Zi. The actual Chinese text can quite literally say,

> It's not possible for all in the world to understand [my teachings], and so it's not possible for everyone [in the world] to practice them.

Lao Zi, on one hand, is simply noting that these teachings are rarely heard and understood by anyone (and in his day this would have been quite true), so few people could possibly have followed him and practiced his teachings However, the meaning of this verse goes deeper than this, as he also understood that people are easily distracted from the states of clarity and tranquility. So, he said that his teachings are not understood nor put into practice because he acknowledged people's attachments to the Three Poisons, Six-Sense Desires, and Seven Emotions.

Wei wu wei is it at the heart of Daoist philosophy, being a central theme of the *Dao De Jing, Zhuang Zi,* and *Lei Zi.* Practicing the three ideals of non-contention, noninterference, and nonconformity are then the ways of incorporating this principle of active non-action into your daily life, grounding you in Daoist philosophy.

The effects of practicing wei wu wei on yourself, others, and the world is like the analogy of throwing a pebble into a still pond, the ripple effects spread across the entire surface, just as these acts of cultivation affect the way people interact with each other. Daoism asserts that we can bring more positive change to our world through our silent examples than by voicing loud opinions of how people should act and live.

1) Active Non-Contention (為 無 爭, **Wei Wu Zheng**)
In the *Clarity and Tranquility of the Constant Scripture,* Lao Zi states, "The superior person does not contend. The inferior person is quarrelsome." He also says, "Because I contend with no one, no one can contend with me." Being conscious of not contending is active non-contention. Guarding speech is one way in which Daoists are always mindful of preventing acts of contending. Contentious words and actions have a habit of rebounding on the speaker. Actually, most of the time we contend with others, either in minor or major ways. Some people do not contend overtly, but instead use passive aggression or other means of contending indirectly. Usually our egos will not allow us to react to or hear anything contradictory without some sort of contention. For example, if someone says something that we don't agree with, we might tense up, roll our

eyes, or sigh heavily. Our body language reveals our thoughts, and our thoughts are often filled with contention.

An old Chinese saying advises, "When being praised, act as if being blamed. When being blamed, act as though being praised." Normally when being blamed for something, we tend to redirect the blame elsewhere, at times becoming defensive and sometimes attacking those who criticized us. On the other hand, most of us appreciate being praised. We often desire it, and in extreme cases, demand it. But if you think about it, we have to ask ourselves, why do people praise us? Do they want something? Equally, when people blame us, it would be wise to consider the possibility that they might be right.

This saying encourages us to follow the middle way when experiencing blame or praise. It should not be taken literally as a fixed response to every incident of blame or praise, rather keeping this saying in mind creates a mindset for non-contention, leads to a more balanced perspective within our interactions, and raises the consciousness to think more clearly in these kinds of situations. Seeing the opportunity to grow from criticism—either because it has some truth and you can learn from it, or, when it's not true, you have the opportunity to rise above it—is a much more beneficial way to approach criticism in our lives. As Li Qingyun stated on this subject,

> No one can know when either praise or criticism will come. To be angry because of people's criticism or to be happy about praise are both emotional defects. The emotions will thus make you uneasy. Sensible persons will grin and bear criticism, and refuse praise politely. Then the mind will be calm and clear like a mirror.

(*The Immortal: True Accounts of the 250-Year-Old Man, Li Qingyun* by Yang Sen.)

In the case of dealing with people who commit hostile and slanderous transgressions (this is the type of person whom Lao Zi called the "lesser minded" or "inferior person") it serves no good purpose to either respond or attack in kind, rather it is far more effective to embrace non-contention, showing calmness and clarity in the midst of such contentious situations. In conjunction with this, Lao Zi says in chapter 68 of the *Dao De Jing,* "A good fighter does not act with anger." This does not just apply to martial artists or soldiers, it applies to anyone in a situation of contention.

In chapter 49 of the *Dao De Jing,* Lao Zi also states, "To the good, I am good to them. To the not good, I am also good to them. This is the virtue of goodness." In this statement Lao Zi is not advising that we allow people to walk all over, abuse, or take advantage of us, but that we turn the conditions of conflict into conditions of cooperation by not contending with others, whether they be good or not good.

The primary message of Lao Zi's teachings is about non-contention—meaning, to replace the contention inside of us with acceptance, kindness, and trust toward others, so to bring harmony into people's hearts. Constantly expressing non-contention with this purpose in mind culminates into a spiritual power that he called the "virtue of goodness."

Contention can result in aggression, and where there is aggression, there can be no peace. Aggression only leads to anger, resentment, and fear. Daoist philosophy does not advocate using aggression, hostility, revenge, or violence against others because these types of actions only tend to feed upon themselves. As Lao Zi says in chapter 42 of the *Dao De Jing,* "The violent person will die a violent death."

Aggression is not always active—more often than not it is passive. We can react and express anger in many different and subtle ways. In the workplace we can attempt to advance our position or standing through gossip and criticism. In our relationships we can withdraw affection, make sharp retorts, respond coldly when we know it will hurt, and we can be irritable at the slightest annoyance. In the end, it is always best to examine our aggressive behavior through self-reflection rather than only reflecting on the actions of others. This is not to say others don't do things that are wrong, but it is more important to question our own responses and try to understand these situations from the other person's point of view. The world would be far more peaceful and harmonious if everyone would reflect on their own contention and aggression, instead of constantly focusing on the wrongdoings of others.

Chapter 49 warrants repeating here, in its entirety, because it relates well to how the sage exemplifies nonaggression:

The sage has no fixed heart. He takes everyone's heart as his heart. To the good, I am good to them. To the not good, I am also good to them. This is the virtue of goodness. To the trustworthy, I trust them. To the not trustworthy, I also trust them. This is the virtue of trustworthiness. The sage dwelling in the world does so by bringing harmony to people's hearts. The people all raise their eyes and ears because the sage can regard them all as innocent children.

Lao Zi is talking about accepting others for who they are and not reacting with resistance to them. If we accept people and believe they are good and trustworthy, and focus on their good qualities and actions, they will blossom. Daoists believe in teaching and correcting others through acceptance, kindness, trust, and promoting harmony.

The sage accepts people as they are because he treats everyone as an innocent child, and children are at their best when they receive love, acceptance, kindness, and trust. When my teacher advised, "Treat people as though they are eight years old," he was saying to be like the sage and accept people for who they are, and to treat them with the same kindness (and patience) as you would a child.

2) Active Non-Interference (為無擾, Wei Wu Rao)

Before explaining what is meant by noninterference, let's be clear on what it isn't. Noninterference doesn't mean ignoring people harming and injuring others. If a kind and caring person, be they Daoist or not, saw someone hurting a child, for example, they would take action to help the child. This is not interference—it is protection of the innocent.

For people who are being harmful to themselves, but are not harming others, however, the issue isn't so clear. Some people who are heavy drinkers, for example, may be perfectly satisfied with their level of drinking, even though they know it isn't the best thing for their health. Their situation is very different from people who drink to cope with depression or other issues in their life. "Happy alcoholics," though still being harmful to themselves, may resent others trying to interfere with their right to drink, which leads to issues of contention and other problems. On the other hand, for people who are uncomfortable with their amount of drinking and are looking to change, they would be grateful for someone wanting to help. This subject of noninterference, then, can be a little tricky to apply in a fixed manner, but Daoists have a distinct perspective on this principle of non-action.

People, nations, political factions, and religions love to tell others how to live, but Daoists prefer to leave people alone, just as they wish to be left alone. Your Dao may not be my Dao, so why should I interfere?

This Daoist perspective aligns with nature. Many times, for example, I have observed birds sitting on the power lines in my backyard, but I've never yet seen one bird turn to another bird and say that its feathers aren't right, or that it should eat only certain types of seeds. Birds don't exercise rules of propriety toward other birds. Only humans spend time telling others how to behave. Contrary to most human behavior, Daoists seek to be in tune with nature (naturalism), to imitate it (by following the Dao), and to bring harmony into their lives (attaining the Dao).

An old Daoist adage states, "Birds fly, fish swim"—these are the natural ways for birds and fish, and all humans have their natural way as well. The great Daoist philosopher Yang Zhu (陽朱) in the *Lei Zi* says, "The Dao of the ancients was to be in harmony and at peace with everyone." Obviously, we cannot be in harmony and at peace with others if we are interfering in their lives.

One of the main forms of interference is the act of giving unsolicited advice to others. Too often people feel they are the only ones who are right and so feel the need to correct and advise others according to their viewpoint.

As Lao Zi states in chapter 81 of the *Dao De Jing*, "The one who knows does not know all. The one who knows all does not know at all." It is the natural function of our ego causing us to believe that our thoughts, experiences, and viewpoints are objective and correct. This leads us to believe we are doing the right thing by correcting and advising others.

In "Live and Let Live," chapter 6 of the Yang Zhu section in the *Lie Zi*, Yang Zhu tells a story about the ill-outcome of interference through a conversation with Zi Chan, a proud and arrogant ruler of a principality called Zheng. Zheng was prosperous and well protected, and Zi Chan credited himself with all the state's accomplishments, erroneously thinking he knew what was best for everyone. Zi Chan had two brothers, Gong Sunchao, who loved drinking wine and was in a continual state of being inebriated, and Gong Sunmu, who loved women and was continually seeking out females through gift giving and using go-betweens for his amorous inclinations. Zi Chan thought his two brothers were engaged in harmful behaviors. After telling them how he thought they should conduct themselves, his brothers responded,

… are you not just being mean-spirited and pitiful by acting so proud of your achievements in ruling the state? Why do you come to disturb our minds with these erroneous high ideals and attempts to infect us with your grandiose thoughts of fame and profit?

It is now our turn to debate this issue with you. A man who professes to be good at regulating the lives of others rarely succeeds at anything other than overworking and disrupting his own life. But a man who is good at regulating his own life can perceive his own true nature without interfering in the lives of others. Therefore, your way of regulating others might work for ruling a state, but is out of sync with what lies in a person's heart. On the other hand, our way of regulating ourselves can be applied to everyone and can bring an end to this way of a ruler and those who serve him. For so long we attempted by example to help you understand our way of living, instead you just come here to preach your way to us.

At first, this text starts out sounding like a moral injunction against drinking and womanizing, but it turns into a story about the problems of excessive ego and interfering with others. Zi Chan made the error of interfering with how his two brothers wanted to live, but his greatest error was in touting his own accomplishments and believing he was above his brothers.

Living with aggression and interfering with others causes people to focus on petty issues, becoming blinded to what is really important—the nurturing of their own life and spirit. Just as we saw with Zi Chan, he was so involved in the issues of running a state, he forgot about what really matters. Nurturing your own life and spirit means to be more mindful of them, which keeps you focused on yourself, and helps you to allow others to follow their Dao. Interfering and being aggressive, for the most part, is about controlling others—trying to get them to conform to your beliefs—this takes them away from their path. Nurturing your own life and spirit is developed by living according to wei wu wei (active non-action).

It does no good to interfere with others by telling them what to do (often this takes the form of "do as I say, not as I do"). When someone tells us what to do (even if we are asking for advice), we normally find ways to resist. However, when we see a behavior or discipline in others that we wish to emulate, we become inspired to practice it. We gladly and enthusiastically adopt it.

When I was young, and my mother asked me to rake leaves, for example, I was reluctant and usually did a poor job. I considered raking to be a chore and felt my mother was interfering in my playtime. But when my friends wanted to rake up a big pile of leaves so we could jump into it, my attitude toward raking greatly changed. Seeing my friends so enthusiastically raking made me enjoy the activity. My mother caught on to this and would start raking and tell me she was making a big pile so I could play in it. My heart would jump and I'd happily join in on the raking from then on.

3) Active Non-Conformity (為無遵, Wei Wu Zun)

The idea of nonconformity doesn't mean to do everything the opposite of what everyone else is doing. Rather, it is about following what you know to be your path (Dao) in life. Doing what others expect you to do, especially when it conflicts with what is in your heart, creates conditions of discontentment, anger, and confusion. To be actively nonconforming means to do what you feel is right and to follow your own path, even if others don't approve.

Conformity is usually a matter of people allowing conditions to turn them, rather than them turning conditions. You could be getting ready to meditate, for example, and a friend will call and say, "Let's go out to eat." Being "turned by conditions" means foregoing the meditation and going out to eat. "Turning conditions" is telling the friend you would be happy to go eat, after you finish meditating.

Nonconformity in Daoism is truly about listening to your own self, to your intuition. Listening and abiding by your heart means listening to your inner self, not just seeking the advice of others. In chapter 2 of the *Zhuang Zi,* Zhuang Zhou states,

> If one abided by their own heart and treated it as their teacher, who then would be the only one without a teacher?

This quote isn't saying we should not have teachers or read books, but what we learn from teachers and books must be processed through our own intuition.

My teacher said, "If you believe entirely in teachers, better not have teachers. If you believe entirely in books, better not have books." To do so is just conforming to the ideas of others, not your own true self.

Master Liang recognized that not everything a teacher or book says may be useful to you. We must take from them what applies to us, and not just blindly follow. So, to learn from many teachers and read many books is helpful when trying to find your Personal Dao, but this is no more than having the doorway pointed out to you. Going through the door, however, can only be done by you.

Nonconformity in the view of Daoism is not about just doing whatever you please or disregarding responsibilities. To do so will just create problems and discord in your life. The ideal of nonconformity is to lead the life you wish for yourself. Whether you want to be married and have children, become a monk or nun, be a scientist, make art, practice medicine, defend the law, or study nature—no matter what path you wish to follow in life, it takes sincerity and an unwavering commitment to produce a good result.

As stated in *The Heavenly Worthy's Jade Pivot Treasury Scripture* (天尊玉樞寶經, Tian Zun Yu Shu Bao Jing), "It takes sincerity to enter the Dao." So, by extension, it takes sincerity to embark upon your path. In the Daoist view, the very meaning of being an active nonconformist means to follow your path (not the expectations of others) and then commit to where your path leads you (and not be distracted by the wishes of others).

You and the Dao are not two separate things, they are one in the same. When we realize this, we are, as Lao Zi says, "transformed," and transformation is about people finding their Way and then following it. To undergo transformation means to change. People may like to think they are already pretty good and don't need to change, but this is because change is difficult and no one really likes it. But as Master Liang said, "Those who don't think they need to change will be forever lost and without the Dao."

Life is full of decisions, and setting out to find our Personal Dao is one of the biggest decisions we make in life. But to make this particular decision, we must have an awareness and clear understanding of the negative influences of the Three Poisons, Six Sense Desires, and the Seven Emotions because they will just lead us to conformity and distraction, not to our own true self.

The Way of Sincerity, Silence, and Gentleness

The Heavenly Worthy's Jade Pivot Treasury Scripture truly summarizes what being a Daoist is all about when it states,
> It takes sincerity to enter into the Dao.
> It takes silence to guard it.
> It takes gentleness to use it.

Every student of the Dao should pay close attention to this quote. If we are not sincere about our cultivation, the spirit cannot develop. If we don't guard our speech, the vitality will dissipate. If we aren't gentle, the essence will be damaged. Sincerity, silence, and gentleness are like the three supporting legs of a cauldron in which the Three Treasures (of essence/jing, vitality/qi, and spirit/shen) are forged together into what Daoists call the "elixir"—which is none other than a fully realized, awakened, and illuminated spirit.

Spirit (shen) relies on sincerity as it cannot come forth (to be realized, awakened, or illuminated) unless there is an unwavering resolve to realize and awaken it, and an unquestioning knowing of a bright spirit within. This bright spirit is the Original Spirit, located in a person's lower abdomen, which can only come forth if absolute focus is put upon it, and when vitality (qi) and essence (jing) are replenished adequately enough to nurture it.

So, to enter the Dao we need to be sincere in our actions and intents. When we are truly sincere, we experience no distraction, no wavering, and no confusion. Sincerity is like a direct connection with our higher self (the Hun, or Heavenly spirit), and the lower self (Po, Earthly spirit) can gain no foothold.

The qi relies on silence, an internal calmness so the breath may come into fullness. Daoism normally calls this "guarding the speech," because it is through the mouth that qi is dissipated. With too much talk the breath is agitated and so it cannot accumulate nor can it be mobilized in the body. This is why Daoists try to speak only when necessary, when their words can be useful, and they do so with a softness, like a gentle breeze. Being silent and guarding the speech is the key to accumulating qi.

Essence relies on gentleness, which has three meanings: First is to avoid excessively toiling or taxing the body. Second is to properly nourish the body so as not to overwork the processes of the internal organs. Third is for men to avoid dissipating their sexual energy and releasing secretions too excessively, and for women to ingest herbs and undertake practices for lessening the menstrual flow. Being gentle with the body and its functions is how we accumulate and replenish our jing (essence). As Lao Zi says in chapter 52 of the *Dao De Jing,* "Do nothing to harm the body." This doesn't mean we shouldn't exercise the body, work, or engage in sexual activity. It means that we should not be excessive about exercise, work, and sexual activity. Moderation is the best solution. Through moderation, we are being gentle with ourselves.

In applying the actions of sincerity, silence, and gentleness, we come full circle with Lao Zi's Three Treasures discussed in the first chapter. Kindness can only truly occur within sincerity, silence is an action of frugality, and gentleness is an expression of humility. So when we examine these three words of sincerity, silence, and gentleness, and consider their importance in Daoism, we can see why the myriad Daoist practices are so rooted in yin energy. Meditation is a yin activity, as are the Eight Brocades Seated Qigong exercises, taijiquan, and all the other various Daoist exercises and martial art styles. They all make use of energy relying on the promotion of yin, and on the principles of sincerity, silence, and gentleness. In chapter 78 of the *Dao De Jing,* Lao Zi says,

Nothing in the world is softer and weaker than water.
Yet, in overcoming the hard and strong, nothing can compare to it.

In Daoism, then, the underlying intention is to be like water—flowing, gentle, yielding, and all-encompassing. The hard and inflexible breaks, deteriorating quickly because it is unyielding. So if we wish to enter the Dao, to guard the Dao, and make use of the Dao, we need to cultivate within ourselves the three principles of sincerity, silence, and gentleness. In doing this, we are at our most perfect state of being because we are like water.

Just as the Chinese character for Dao shows a person drifting along with the current of a watercourse way, being and flowing like water is *Being Daoist*.

Afterword

I have no doubt that this book will create as many questions about Daoism as it has answered. To help fill any gaps in information, please refer to the suggested reading sections throughout this work, and especially to the three books listed below, which provide a clear and broad understanding of Daoism, while rendering very insightful accounts of Daoist life during the early 1900s. As mentioned in my introduction, it's difficult to define Daoism in any precise manner. In my view, however, Daoism is a philosophy that can only be truly understood when it is evidenced by living in accord with one's Personal Dao. There is a deep beauty to Daoism, a profound gentleness, and grace of simplicity that cannot be discovered by books or teachers alone. The inherent naturalism and spirituality of Daoism needs to be sought through our own inner reflection and realization of the immortal spirit within us. Attain clarity and tranquility, and you will realize the meaning of Daoism.

Recommended Reading:

- *Taoism: The Road to Immortality* by John Blofeld (Shambhala, 1978).
- *The Immortal: True Accounts of the 250-Year-Old Man, Li Qingyun* by Yang Sen, translated by Stuart Alve Olson (Valley Spirit Arts, 2014).
- *The Monastery of Jade Mountain* by Peter Goullart (Llanerch Publishers, 1961).

About the Author

Stuart Alve Olson, longtime protégé of Master T.T. Liang (1900–2002), is a teacher, translator, and writer on Daoist philosophy, health, and internal arts. Since his early twenties, he has studied and practiced Daoism and Chinese Buddhism.

As of 2013, Stuart has published eighteen books, many of which now appear in several foreign-language editions. He is currently working on completing the entire Chen Kung Series with revised editions of earlier works as well as new volumes on sections he has never previously published.

Stuart has performed numerous book signings, appeared on many TV and radio talk shows throughout the United States, written several articles for martial art and Daoist magazines, and has taught Daoism and taijiquan in Taiwan, Hong Kong, Indonesia, Canada, and Italy.

Stuart was voted the 2012 *IMOS Journal* Reader's Choice Award for "Best Author on Qigong."

He currently lives in Phoenix, Arizona, with his wife, Lily.

Brief Biography

On Christmas Day, 1979, Stuart took Triple Refuge with Chan Master Hsuan Hua, receiving the disciple name Kuo Ao. In 1981, he participated in the meditation sessions and sutra lectures given by Dainin Katagiri Roshi at the Minnesota Center for Zen Meditation. In late 1981, he began living with Master Liang, studying taijiquan, Daoism, Praying Mantis kung fu, and Chinese language under his tutelage.

In the spring of 1982 through 1984, Stuart undertook a two-year Buddhist bowing pilgrimage, "Nine Steps, One Bow." Traveling along state and county roads during the spring, summer, and autumn months, starting from the Minnesota Zen Meditation Center in Minneapolis and ending at the border of Nebraska. During the winter months he stayed at Liang's home and bowed in his garage.

After Stuart's pilgrimage, he returned to Liang's home to continue studying with him. He and Master Liang then started traveling throughout the United States teaching taijiquan to numerous groups, and continued to do so for nearly a decade.

In 1986, Stuart published his first four books on taijiquan —*Wind Sweeps Away the Plum Blossoms, Cultivating the Ch'i, T'ai Chi Sword, Sabre & Staff*, and *Imagination Becomes Reality.*

In 1987, Stuart made his first of several trips to China, Taiwan, and Hong Kong. On subsequent trips, he studied massage in Taipei and taught taijiquan in Taiwan and Hong Kong.

In 1989, he and Master Liang moved to Los Angeles, where Stuart studied Chinese language and continued his taijiquan studies.

In early 1992, Stuart made his first trip to Indonesia, where he was able to briefly study with the kung-fu and healing master Oei Kung Wei. He also taught taijiquan there to many large groups.

In 1993, he organized the Institute of Internal Arts in St. Paul, Minnesota, and brought Master Liang back from California to teach there.

In 2005, Stuart was prominently featured in the British taijiquan documentary *Embracing the Tiger*.

In 2006, he formed Valley Spirit Arts with his longtime student Patrick Gross.

In 2010, he began teaching for the Sanctuary of Dao and writing for its blog and newsletter.

In 2012, Stuart received the IMOS Journal Reader's Choice Award for "Best Author on Qigong."

Body of Works
Daoism
- *Tao of No Stress: Three Simple Paths* (Healing Arts Press, 2002).
- *Qigong Teachings of a Taoist Immortal: The Eight Essential Exercises of Master Li Ching-Yun (Healing Arts Press, 2002).*
- *The Jade Emperor's Mind Seal Classic: The Taoist Guide to Health, Longevity, and Immortality* (Inner Traditions, 2003).

Forthcoming Books
- *The Immortal: True Accounts of the 250-Year-Old Man, Li Qingyun* by Yang Sen (Valley Spirit Arts, 2014).
- *Clarity and Tranquility: A Daoist Guide on the Meditation Practice of Tranquil Sitting* (Valley Spirit Arts, 2014).
- *Refining the Elixir: The Internal Alchemy Teachings of Daoist Immortal Zhang Sanfeng* (Valley Spirit Arts, 2014). (Daoist Immortal Three Peaks Zhang Series).

- *Seen and Unseen: A Daoist Guide for the Meditation Practice of Inner Contemplation* (Valley Spirit Arts, 2014).
- *The Yellow Emperor's Yin Convergence Scripture* (Valley Spirit Arts, 2014).
- *The Actions and Retribution Treatise* (Valley Spirit Arts, 2015).
- **The Book of Sun and Moon—Volume One** *Traditional Perspectives on Divination and Calculation of the* Book of Changes (Valley Spirit Arts, 2015).
- **The Book of Sun and Moon—Volume Two** *Interpreting the 64 Images of the* Book of Changes (Valley Spirit Arts, 2015).
- **The Book of Sun and Moon—Volume Three** *The Logic and Creation of the 64 Images of the* Book of Changes (Valley Spirit Arts, 2015).
- **The Book of Sun and Moon—Volume Four** *The Ten Wings of the* Book of Changes (Valley Spirit Arts, 2015).

Taijiquan Books
- *T'ai Chi Thirteen Sword: A Sword Master's Manual* (Unique Publications, 1999).
- *T'ai Chi for Kids: Move with the Animals*, illustrated by Gregory Crawford (Bear Cub Books, 2001).
- *Steal My Art—The Life and Times of Tai Chi Master T.T. Liang* (North Atlantic Books, 2002).
- *T'ai Chi According to the I Ching—Embodying the Principles of the Book of Changes* (Healing Arts Press, 2002).
- *Imagination Becomes Reality: 150-Posture Taijiquan of Master T.T. Liang* (Valley Spirit Arts, 2011).

- *Tai Ji Quan Treatise: Attributed to the Song Dynasty Daoist Priest Zhang Sanfeng* (Valley Spirit Arts, 2011).

(Daoist Immortal Three Peaks Zhang Series)
- *The Wind Sweeps Away the Plum Blossoms: Yang Style Taijiquan Staff and Spear Techniques* (Valley Spirit Arts, 2011).

Chen Kung Series
- *Tai Ji Qi: Fundamentals of Qigong, Meditation, and Internal Alchemy,* vol. 1 (Valley Spirit Arts, 2013).
- *Tai Ji Jin: Discourses on Intrinsic Energies for Mastery of Self-Defense Skills,* vol. 2 (Valley Spirit Arts, 2013).
- *Tai Ji Bing Shu: Mastering the Arts of Sword, Saber, and Staff Weapon Skills,* vol. 6 (Valley Spirit Arts, 2014).

Forthcoming Books
- *Tai Ji Quan: Practice and Philosophy of the 108-Posture Solo Form,* vol. 3 (Valley Spirit Arts, 2015).
- *Tai Ji Tui Shou & Da Lu: Mastering the Eight Operations of Sensing Hands and Greater Rolling-Back,* vol. 4 (Valley Spirit Arts, 2014).
- *Tai Ji San Shou: Dispersing Hands Exercises for Mastering Intrinsic Energies Skills,* vol. 5 (Valley Spirit Arts, 2015).

Kung-Fu
- *The Complete Guide to Northern Praying Mantis Kung Fu* (Blue Snake Books, 2010).

Forthcoming Book
- *18 Lohan Exercises* (Valley Spirit Arts, 2014).

Check out Stuart's author page at Amazon:
www.amazon.com/author/stuartalveolson

About the Publisher

Valley Spirit Arts offers books and DVDs on Daoism, taijiquan, and meditation practices primarily from author Stuart Alve Olson, longtime student of Master T.T. Liang and translator of many Daoist-related works.

Its website provides teachings on meditation and internal alchemy, taijiquan, qigong, and kung fu through workshops, private and group classes, and online courses and consulting.

For more information as well as updates on Stuart Alve Olson's upcoming projects and events, please visit: www.valleyspiritarts.com

About the Sanctuary of Dao

Established in 2010, the Sanctuary of Dao is a nonprofit organization dedicated to the sharing of Daoist philosophy and practices through online resources, yearly meditation retreats, and community educational programs. The underlying mission of the Sanctuary of Dao is to bring greater health, longevity, and contentment to its members and everyone it serves.

Please visit sanctuaryofdao.org for more information about the organization and its programs.

CPSIA information can be obtained at www.ICGtesting.com
Printed in the USA
LVOW11s1627150814

399348LV00008B/1037/P